GIVE
SMART

GIVE
$MART

PHILANTHROPY
THAT GETS RESULTS

Thomas J. Tierney
Joel L. Fleishman

WITH NAN STONE

PublicAffairs
New York

Editorial production by *Marra*thon Production Services. www.marrathon.net
Design by Jane Raese
Set in 12.5-point Garamond 3

Library of Congress Cataloging-in-Publication Data
Tierney, Thomas J.
Give smart : philanthropy that gets results / Thomas J. Tierney and Joel L.
  Fleishman.
p. cm.
Includes bibliographical references and index.
ISBN 978-1-58648-895-6 — ISBN 978-1-58648-989-2 (e-book)
1. Charities—United States. 2. Nonprofit organizations—United States.
I. Fleishman, Joel L. II. Title.
HV91.T54   2011
361.7'4—dc22
2010047317

First Edition
10 9 8 7 6 5 4 3 2 1

For Eleanor and Ralph Tierney,
who shaped my values and beliefs
while teaching me always to do my share—
and then some.

~Tom

To my parents, A. M. and Ruth Fleishman.
My memory of their example will always inspire me
to strive to be a blessing for others.

~Joel

CONTENTS

PREFACE

We believe that you *can* achieve significantly greater results with the money and time you give away—*if* you put your mind where your heart inclines you, *if* you confront the right questions, and *if* you are willing to try. In those three "ifs" lies the key to unlocking philanthropy's full potential—for donors and for foundations.

We believe that all philanthropy is deeply personal and highly circumstantial. There are no simple steps, fancy frameworks, or trusted tools upon which you can always rely. We believe that by asking the right questions—at the right time and in the right way—you will be far more likely to achieve the change you want to bring about in the world. You will also have a lot more fun, and live a richer and more meaningful life.

These beliefs led us to create this book. With it, our primary goal is to serve those who serve society, and to do so in a manner that will help them achieve genuinely better results for their communities, their countries, and our world. Whom do we have in mind? First, everyone engaged in the work of giving: individual donors and their families, foundation executives, philanthropic advisors, trustees, and decision makers of every sort who are motivated to Give Smart—to use their own philanthropic resources or those they steward to generate the best possible results. We expect this book will also prove useful for people on the receiving end of philanthropic giving:

the leaders of the mission-driven organizations that constitute the world of philanthropy's "grantees."

The ideas presented in these pages are the product of our personal and institutional experiences. They bridge theory and practice, business and academia, grant making and grant receiving. In a very real sense, this book is the endpoint to a journey we embarked upon from quite different starting points. One of us, Tom, began in the business world, where he pursued a career in management consulting that culminated in his becoming worldwide managing director of Bain & Company; he served on the boards of many nonprofits along the way. And one of us, Joel, began in academia, where he produced new knowledge about foundations and their charitable giving; he ultimately served as founder and faculty chair of the Center for Strategic Philanthropy and Civil Society at Duke University's Sanford School of Public Policy.

Our separate journeys converged about fifteen years ago, when Joel was president of the Atlantic Philanthropies' U.S. Program Staff. Joel adamantly encouraged Tom to pursue his dream of creating a nonprofit professional services organization that could help social sector organizations improve their performance, much as Bain & Company had helped (and continues to help) its corporate clients succeed. That encouragement, and Atlantic Philanthropies' cornerstone funding, gave birth to The Bridgespan Group, an independent nonprofit that spun out of its incubation at Bain & Company in 2000. It has since engaged in an array of initiatives aimed at helping individuals and organizations achieve breakthrough results on society's behalf.

One of the ways in which Bridgespan pursues its mission is by working with hundreds of nonprofits—in fields ranging from education to environment to community development—assisting service providers, advocacy organizations, and intermediaries. At the same time, Bridgespan also works closely with philanthropists and foundations, thus bridging the gap between those who give and those who receive. The insights sparked by this dual perspective have informed and shaped Tom's thinking. This book builds on his essay "Toward Higher-Impact Philanthropy," published in 2006 in *Taking Philanthropy Seriously*.[1]

Meanwhile, Joel has pursued his own passion: working to make philanthropists, and especially foundations, more effective in their charitable giving. His efforts culminated in 2007 with the publication of *The Foundation: A Great American Secret* and an accompanying casebook, which together comprise a record of how philanthropy has been practiced in the United States since the early years of the twentieth century.

As each of us was pursuing his own path, we continued to talk and compare notes. Gradually, we realized that our experiences were highly complementary: Joel focusing on the foundations that funded grantees' proposals and Bridgespan serving many of those same grantees, as well as an ever-broader array of individual philanthropists. Our thinking, too, was highly compatible, and we began discussing a book that might bring our experience and views together in one compact volume.

You hold the result in your hands.

Readers will quickly discover that this book has two central biases: a bias toward content essential for decision making and a bias toward the *pragmatic*—toward ideas that have proven useful in the real world. We work with and admire academics, consultants, policy makers, and students of the social sector, but this book is aimed explicitly at people who have the awesome responsibility of *giving money away and not having it anymore* while, at the same time, achieving the best possible results. This isn't easy, and those people deserve the best possible thinking.

Every book can be improved. Our hope is that you will not only find our work useful but also add your ideas and views. Philanthropy, once the most stately of endeavors, has evolved into a dynamic enterprise, and new insights are constantly emerging from across the social sector and around the globe. We are eager to hear how *your* version of philanthropy is evolving. To that end, please join us in updating and adding to these ideas through the Bridgespan Web site (www. bridgespan.org/givesmart) so that the journey can continue and broaden.

Thomas J. Tierney
Chairman, The Bridgespan Group

Joel Fleishman
Professor of Law and Public Policy, Duke University

INTRODUCTION

FROM ASPIRATIONS
TO IMPACT

I'm giving away money—some would say lots of money. And yet it pales in comparison to the needs I see all around me: urban slums and rural poverty, children in failing schools and children without access to any schooling whatsoever, deforestation and unclean water, crippling diseases of many kinds. The needs are immense, at home and abroad. My aspirations are so much greater than my resources that at times it feels as though I'm trying to hold back the tide. I want my giving to do the most it can . . . but how?

W E HAVE HEARD THESE SENTIMENTS FROM every corner of the philanthropic universe, across America and around the world. They are echoed by experienced donors giving away hundreds of millions a year and rookies with newly established donor-advised funds; by families engaged in private foundations, as well as by their independent trustees and advisors; by all manner of foundation decision makers, from chief executives to program officers. The speakers' roles and circumstances vary widely, but they share the aspiration to get the most from their philanthropy—

and a nagging concern that they could indeed accomplish more.

The concern is warranted. Every donor wants his or her money to make a difference, and nobody wants to see hard-earned wealth (their own or a benefactor's) go to waste. Yet philanthropy's natural state is underperformance. The generosity that causes people to use their wealth on others' behalf is a wonderful expression of humanity at its best, and it can bring enormous joy into a donor's life. But generosity alone is rarely sufficient if you aspire to leave a legacy of exceptional results. Outstanding philanthropy is distinguished by what it achieves as well as by the act of charity itself. It requires you to complement your heartfelt generosity with a disciplined consideration of what you hope to accomplish: the results that will define success, what it will take to achieve them, and how those results will get better over time.

This rigorous approach to how you practice philanthropy is what we mean when we say, "Give smart." It may sound unexceptional. In practice, it is much less straightforward—and far more valuable—than it may first appear.

PHILANTHROPY'S "TERRIBLE TRUTHS"

Giving money away is easy. If you can sign your name at the bottom of a check, or approve the slate of grants at a family foundation board meeting, or accept proposals from aspiring grantees, you can give money away. Giving it away smartly, so that it not only gets results but also gets more and better results over time, is hard. In addition to the sheer difficulty of the issues many philanthropists choose to tackle, you also have to reckon with some "terrible truths" that are rooted in the realities of how the social sector works: All philanthropy is personal. Results can confound. Excellence is self-imposed.

All philanthropy is personal. In the United States alone, there are more than one million nonprofit organizations engaged in every sort of activity, from promoting the arts to organizing zoological expeditions. This diverse and dynamic landscape is the product of the freedom enjoyed by individuals and foundations to support whatever causes they care most about. This same freedom also explains why, quite understandably, not all philanthropic giving is motivated purely or even primarily by the desire to achieve results.

All philanthropy is personal and, as donors, we make gifts for many different reasons: responsibilities to our communities or colleagues ("doing my share"), personal relationships ("can't say no"), giving back, returning a favor, fulfilling our volunteer commitments ("we need 100 percent participation from the board"). Such gifts may be relatively small, given our circumstances, or they may be substantial, as evidenced by the large number of six-, seven-, and even eight-figure gifts given to educational, medical, and cultural institutions each year. Either way, the motivation behind the gift is primarily personal. Results matter, of course, but results are not the driving force.

When institutions replace individuals as the source of funds, philanthropy's personal taproots do not disappear, even if they are seldom discussed publicly. In family-run foundations, trustees naturally feel a certain sense of ownership of the institution's assets, and their interests and worldviews are likely to influence the focus and nature of its grants. Professionally staffed foundations typically have well-defined institutional priorities and processes, yet their program managers often have considerable discretionary latitude in proposing grants, as do the executive directors who ultimately decide what will go before the board. Since many of these individuals are recruited on the basis of their expertise and experience, institutional confidence in their judgment is not at all surprising. But neither should it be surprising that many day-to-day decisions bear their personal stamp.

Results can confound. In the complex world of giving money away, tangible philanthropy—funding the construction of a new marine biology laboratory for instance, or buying up conservation land—is about as straightforward as it gets. As donors, we can take pride in our contributions without worrying that we may not have gotten quite what we paid for. In contrast, the results of other philanthropic initiatives—funding an after-school tutoring program, sponsoring research on global warming, supporting a local neighborhood's revitalization—can be defiantly difficult to pin down. We bet that such gifts and grants will "make a difference." But unlike a construction site, we cannot easily see the work in progress, nor can we be certain that whatever results we do see are directly attributable to our efforts.

In addition, feedback on the results of our philanthropic efforts can be ambiguous, even suspect. When you are in the business of giving away money, people have a tendency to tell you what they think you want to hear. Surrounded by smiling faces and awash in reassuring rhetoric, it's natural for even the most objective and disciplined donors to think they are really achieving outstanding results. Personal incentives are surreptitiously aligned: givers want to feel good about their contributions; current and potential recipients of those funds need to be liked if they hope to secure future funding. Without hard facts to help, even the most well-intentioned individuals can easily be overwhelmed.

Excellence is self-imposed. This is the last and most terrible truth of all: philanthropy has no built-in systemic forces to motivate continuous improvement. The absence of external accountability is what gives philanthropy its freedom to experiment, take risks, and pursue long-term initiatives on society's behalf. At the same time, it also means that if you do not demand excellence of yourself no one else will require it of you.

Unlike business leaders, philanthropists have no market dynamics with which to contend. There are no competitors fighting to take market share away from them, no customers who will take their money elsewhere if they fail to deliver, no shareholders poised to dump their stock. Nor do they need to answer to the public, as politicians ultimately must. Quite the contrary: grant making is often accomplished through foundations established in perpetuity, insulated (and isolated) from any external pressure other than being required to abide by regulatory and tax laws.

In this Galapagos Island–like world, where there are no natural predators, philanthropy is inclined to persist, but not to excel. Therefore, whether you are a donor, a trustee, or a foundation officer, if you want to narrow the gap between your aspirations and the results your giving achieves, you must be willing to set your own standard of excellence and hold yourself accountable for meeting it.

This is no small challenge. Self-imposed accountability is not a natural act. It requires extraordinary determination and discipline to pursue outstanding results year after year, when nothing in the surrounding environment requires you to do so. It is especially unnatural when you are tackling complicated issues, where there are no proven strategies and results are difficult to assess. Helping to change the life of a child born into poverty or forestall the effects of global warming is fundamentally harder than making the proverbial widget. And yet, examples of philanthropic excellence most certainly exist. As an illustration, consider the stellar results of the partnership between the Fisher family and the Knowledge Is Power Program Foundation, better known as KIPP.

DORIS AND DON FISHER: GETTING AN "A" IN PHILANTHROPY

In 1969, Doris and Don Fisher opened the first Gap clothing store in San Francisco. Frustrated by never being able to find pants that fit Don properly, they went to the root of the problem and began selling their own apparel. Thus, with one pair of pants, a retail sensation was born, and Gap (named by Doris) has since grown to 3,100 stores around the world.

When Don Fisher stepped down as CEO of Gap in 1995, he and Doris began looking for ways to increase their involvement in philanthropy. Don had a long-standing commitment to helping children, honed by more than thirty years of service on the board of the Boys & Girls Club of San Francisco. He was becoming increasingly concerned, as was Doris, about what was happening (or not) in the public schools of the city where he'd grown up. "The interest Doris and I have in improving public education comes from our worry that the gulf is growing, not as much between the 'haves' and 'have-nots' anymore, but between the 'knows' and the 'know-nots,'" Don reflected.[1]

To the Fishers, public charter schools, which offered greater freedom over hiring, budgets, and leadership, seemed to offer the best opportunity to tackle the huge problems facing education. They had another advantage as well: successful efforts could be copied around the country. Rather than support dozens of separate, individual charter schools, the Fishers sought a program where they could use their formidable marketing skills and business experience to help it grow. "I want to do something that's scalable," Don commented, "where we can touch a lot of kids."[2]

Having clarified what they hoped to achieve, Don and Doris next sought advice. They were personally invested and interested in education, but they also knew they had a lot to learn. To that end, they hired Scott Hamilton, then the Massachusetts associate commissioner of education for charter schools, to help them identify high-potential organizations. After a full year of searching and learning, they narrowed their focus to the Knowledge Is Power Program.

At the time, KIPP was just two middle schools in Houston and New York City, but it fit the Fishers' criteria on every dimension. It had a strong, results-oriented approach. Expectations for students were high: the organization had a compelling focus on making college the goal for all students. And the visionary cofounders, Mike Feinberg and Dave Levin, had solid ideas about how to spread the KIPP approach to other cities.

Beyond these many qualifications, however, KIPP had something equally important. It inspired Doris and Don Fisher, because it resonated with their own deeply held values and beliefs, in particular, the belief that race or income shouldn't limit a child's chance to be educated.

Having invested the time to find the right organization, the Fishers were prepared to play a significant role. They committed $15 million over three years to start the KIPP Foundation, designed to help KIPP begin growing toward national scale. In addition, through their frequent communication with KIPP's leaders, they began to realize that more would be needed to make a real difference in the students' lives—first and foremost the right teachers and principals. So when the Fishers learned that, like Feinberg and Levin, two-thirds of the KIPP principals were alumni of Teach for America (TFA), they increased their commitment to help that organization grow as well. Today, 28 percent of KIPP teachers are TFA teachers or alumni. The Fishers also worked with KIPP to launch and fund the Fisher Fellowship, a yearlong leadership-development program with intensive coursework, residencies, and coaching, designed to prepare individuals to open and lead high-performing KIPP schools. Through programs like this, KIPP has developed and retained its best faculty; 73 percent of KIPP school leaders began as KIPP teachers.

Relentlessly seeking results, the Fishers and KIPP strove to learn what was working and what wasn't through transparent sharing of real results. If bad news came, they wanted it unvarnished. KIPP's public, annual report card, which publishes the results of every KIPP school, was Don Fisher's idea.

The results speak for themselves. Since the KIPP Foundation was established in 2000, KIPP has grown to ninety-nine schools in twenty states plus Washington, DC, teaching more than 26,000 students. Moreover, KIPP is nationally recognized as the gold standard in charter education. Of the students who complete eighth grade with KIPP, 95 percent graduate from high school, versus the national average of fewer than 70 percent.[3] Some 88 percent of KIPP eighth-grade completers have gone on to college,[4] far beyond the national average. KIPP is also continuing its ambitious growth, planning to double the number of students served by 2015.[5]

Today, the Fisher family is KIPP's largest national partner,[6] having provided more than $70 million toward the growth of the network—a significant sum, to be sure, but, ultimately, perhaps not as significant as the cumulative time, influence, and leadership they have also given. Don Fisher died in 2009, but Doris continues to support KIPP and their son, John, has succeeded Don as chair of the KIPP Foundation board. This tremendous philanthropic journey, and the opportunity it has created for tens of thousands of young people, began with the strong beliefs of Don and Doris Fisher and their equally strong, self-imposed quest for excellence.

HISTORY LESSONS

Giving smart is not a recent phenomenon. After selling the Carnegie Steel Company to J. P. Morgan in 1901, Andrew Carnegie (aged sixty-six) devoted the remainder of his life to philanthropy. His results ultimately included establishing some twenty-five hundred public libraries, launching the Carnegie Institute of Technology (now Carnegie Mellon University), and building Carnegie Hall in New York City. In

2006, 105 years after Carnegie "repotted" himself, Bill Gates (aged fifty-one) left Microsoft to devote his extraordinary energies to advancing the mission of the Bill & Melinda Gates Foundation. One of its earliest philanthropic initiatives was to install computers in libraries across America. Since then, the foundation has expanded into a wide range of initiatives, from eradicating polio to transforming public education in the United States.

If these two extraordinary philanthropists could compare notes over dinner (we'll assume that Melinda is away on foundation business), they would quickly discover how much they had in common: a relentless ambition to deliver exceptional results through their giving; a deep belief in enabling others to help themselves by leveling the playing field; the willingness to use their brain power, relationships, and influence as well as their money to improve society; the ability to leverage their efforts with other people's money and government support. Rigorous, disciplined, and deeply strategic, the industrial baron and the software tycoon would be highly compatible.

If Gates were to mention "strategic philanthropy," "social entrepreneurs," or "scaling what works" in the course of the conversation, Carnegie might not recognize the phrases, but he would immediately understand the concepts: the need to think hard about your giving, bet on talented people, and pay careful attention to results. A voracious reader, Gates would likewise grasp the continuities, recognizing that language changes faster than principles and that what pass as contemporary insights often fail to appreciate, or fully build upon, relevant lessons from the past.

In fact, when it comes to basic principles, the philanthropy of the industrial era and the philanthropy of the era of nanotechnology are remarkable similar. What is new and constantly evolving is the context within which philanthropists work and the means available to them for getting results. Were Carnegie to spend a few days with the Gateses and their foundation staff, there's no question he would be amazed by the changes from his day to theirs.

Technology is an obvious case in point: the advent of the Internet has enabled all manner of new social-sector business models and tools, from online giving marketplaces like Donors Choose and Kiva, to better methods for measuring and evaluating results. The compounding effect of knowledge is another powerful force: never before has there been so much wealth—or such a wealth of relevant and accessible ideas and information. Changing talent flows that are bringing more people of all ages into careers of public service; new laws and hybrid business-nonprofit models; creative financial structures; blurring boundaries between the sectors: all these and more are creating new opportunities for philanthropists eager to help drive positive change.

Equally important, just as the work that philanthropy does is becoming more global, so are its benefactors. In the years ahead, philanthropists already in the field will increasingly be joined by legions of wealthy contemporaries in India, China, Brazil, and other countries around the globe. Like their predecessors, they will be working in a relentlessly dynamic context, relying upon technologies, tools, and techniques yet to be discovered. And they, too, will be learning some enduring lessons—about the fundamental relationship between thoughtful, considered decision making and philanthropy that gets results; and about the need to avoid the traps that can cause even the most well-intentioned philanthropists to go astray.

TRAPS FOR THE UNWARY

Getting better—steadily better—requires better decisions on every front, from fundamental strategic decisions (like how to define success) to key operational decisions (like whom to hire for a senior staff role). Decisions, after all, are how we allocate resources, and as a donor, your resources—not just your money but also your time and influence—are ultimately the only lever you have to effect change.

The challenge for philanthropists is that many, if not most, of these decisions are often clouded by ambiguity and uncertainty, because the objective data and feedback that could make them more straightforward don't exist, or because they aren't easily available. As a result, more often than not, you're apt to find yourself relying largely if not entirely on your own judgment to make important calls. And that, in turn, means keeping a watchful eye out for some insidious traps that lie in wait at every turn, undermining good intentions and impeding results, even among astonishingly capable and experienced philanthropists.

The first of these traps is *fuzzy headedness*, which occurs when donors allow their emotions and wishful thinking to override logic and thoughtful analysis. Replying to the question "What are you trying to accomplish?" with a response as undefined (and therefore unattainable) as "curing cancer," or "ending poverty," or "stopping global warming" is a common symptom. So is relying on a miracle to get your giving to its desired result: assuming that a $10 million gift can transform an urban school district with an $800 million budget, for example. Another common symptom is falling in love with a charismatic nonprofit leader's plan without examining it through the lens of rational analysis. One consequence of fuzzy headedness is "feel-good" philanthropy, where happy sentiments abound, but the odds of success are small.

The second trap that donors often fall into is *flying solo*. One of philanthropy's great ironies is that very little can be accomplished by individuals acting on their own, even when those individuals are extraordinarily wealthy. The grander your ambitions, the more certain it is that success will require working with and through a broad range of other players, including the nonprofit or nongovernmental organization (NGO) grantees you support; other donors who are passionate about the same issue or issues; government agencies at home or abroad; or members of the public whose views you will have to influence in order to effect change. The list of potential candidates is long and varied. Yet far too many donors and foundation leaders fall prey to trying to go it alone, arrogantly assuming that they have all the answers and can achieve success unilaterally.

The third trap is *underestimating and underinvesting*. It is astonishing how often donors fall into it, given how much philanthropic wealth is created in the high-pressure crucible of business, where mastering the intricacies of finance is essential to survival. The old saying "Everything takes longer and costs more than you expect" holds as true when you are trying to repair the world as it does when you are engaged in home repairs. Yet, as donors, we chronically underestimate what it will actually cost to deliver results and underinvest in the capacity required to make those results a reality.

The consequences of falling into this trap are predictable. The organizations we depend on receive less than they need to perform successfully, and so the next time around we give them even less (or nothing), because they didn't perform as we expected in the first instance. This pattern will persist until more of us are willing to step up as the Fishers did, and say, "You know what? This is going to cost multiple millions of dollars and take years (if not more). So let's not fool ourselves, or those we want to help."

The corollary to this shortfall, and the fourth trap for the unwary, is *nonprofit neglect*. It manifests itself chiefly in philanthropy's widespread resistance to providing general operating support, which grantees can use to develop their organizational capacity. No one likes wasting money, and funding for "overhead" can feel like a waste. But is such money always wasted? Suppose we all decided to fly on the airline that reported the lowest maintenance costs? Or went to the hospitals with the oldest, most depreciated equipment? In many circumstances, consumers gladly pay for more overhead if it delivers value to them.

Nonprofits, too, have good overhead and bad overhead. Paying excessive rent or entertaining lavishly is obviously a waste of money. But what about hiring a chief operating officer who can take on crucial management responsibilities for which the executive director has no time, or a chief financial officer who can develop a long-term funding model to sustain the organization's programs? Are those bad investments? Definitely not, and yet we consistently fall into the trap of believing that nonprofits can deliver A-level results with a malnourished team.

"Prudent" boards of directors make this mistake all the time. They'll have an executive director who is doing a fabulous job of raising money and growing the organization, but is also burning out. And the board will resist funding a chief operating officer, even though it would help the organization sustain its results and ultimately do more, because the position would cost $120,000 a year. Colleagues of ours rightly call the consequences of this trap the "nonprofit starvation cycle."[7]

The starvation cycle is the most egregious manifestation of nonprofit neglect. For the most part, donors' results depend on the performance of the nonprofits they support. Great giving is not accomplished in a vacuum. Yet philanthropists routinely impose an excessive "cost of capital" on their grantees, which erodes the value of their contributions as surely and as imperceptibly as water flowing through a corroded pipe seeps away.

What does this hidden cost of capital look like? It comes in many forms: the philanthropist who thinks he knows how to run an after-school program better than the folks who have been doing just that for twenty-five years and insists on imposing his strategic ideas; the grant maker who annually requires her grantees to fill out fifty-page reports about how the grant was used and what results were achieved, but never acknowledges the reports—and probably never reads them in their entirety. The costs of such behavior in disrupted strategies and unproductive working relationships are real, though rarely tabulated. And because of the enormous power imbalance between those with money and those who need to raise it, they can remain invisible and persist for years on end.

Finally, in a world without competition but overflowing with appreciation and praise, grant makers quite naturally fall into the trap of *satisfactory underperformance*: accepting things as they are without really pushing toward what might be possible. Results are calibrated as "good enough," or perhaps even outstanding, but the motivation to excel, to improve future results by even 10 percent is lacking.

When asked about their relative performance versus that of others, most experienced grant makers would undoubtedly place themselves in the top half of their field (if not the top quartile), a perspective that inevitably nurtures complacency. The only antidote to such complacency is the courage to admit that you could be doing better and the willingness to ask hard questions to that end: "What's working, and what isn't?" "What are other people doing that we could help with or learn from?" "What could we bring to the table besides our money that might help to accelerate and improve results?"

Acknowledging the existence of these traps, and recognizing that they will never really go away, however experienced and wise we become, offers some help in avoiding them. Asking yourself the hard questions we pose below is likely to prove even more helpful, as well as more productive and fun!

QUESTIONS ARE MORE IMPORTANT THAN ANSWERS

In the pages that follow, you will encounter many donors and foundation executives who have turned their philanthropic resources into results, or are striving to do so. Their stories run the gamut from proven successes to works in progress, and they focus on initiatives in fields ranging from education to the environment, human rights to highway safety. Some, like the Rockefeller Foundation's Green Revolution, have entered into history, whereas others, like the Sandler Foundation's ProPublica, are as current as the morning news. Some revolve around new initiatives, such as Connie Duckworth's Arzu, which seeks to empower women and girls in Afghanistan. Others, like Elaine Wynn's engagement with Communities in Schools, underscore the value of investing in the growth of existing high-performing organizations.

These individuals and their stories span decades and demonstrate the wide range of options available to philanthropists. To cite just a few examples, you could choose to work entirely through the grantees you support, or do crucial pieces of the work yourself. Help a small number of high-performing organizations increase the scale of their work, or fund a score of innovative start-ups to help develop a new field. Focus on the needs of your own community, or work with others in lands far away. The varieties are just about limitless. And the basic lesson is clear: there is no one best kind of philanthropy. The path that's right for you will be the one you conceive and design according to your own specific circumstances, ambitions, and values.

There is, however, a smarter way to go about choosing your path. That is to engage in a process of rigorous inquiry around six separate but related questions:

- What are my values and beliefs?
- What is "success" and how can it be achieved?
- What am I accountable for?
- What will it take to get the job done?

- How do I work with grantees?
- Am I getting better?

Taken together, these questions create an approach for donors and grant makers who want to give smart. Wrestling with them will require you to develop strategic clarity, about what you hope to accomplish and what you believe will have to happen for your hopes to be realized, before you leap into action and start making decisions. It will require you to identify a set of results for which you'll hold yourself accountable, so that you can develop real feedback loops for learning and continuing improvement. Last but not least, it will bring you face to face with the harsh realities of what it takes to make change happen when you work with and through nonprofit partners, as well as help you understand how you can be most productive in bettering their performance, and therefore your own.

We have found these questions so powerful in helping donors unlock their philanthropy's potential for delivering results that we have used them as the organizing principle for this book. We recognize that not every question will be equally relevant for every reader, and that their relative importance is likely to change over time, as your circumstances and the arc of your philanthropy evolve. So whether they merit several hours of consideration—or several days, months, or even years—will depend on the specifics of your circumstances as well as on the sum of money involved, the difficulty of the issue (or issues) you're choosing to focus on, and the extent of your ambitions.*

---

*You will find additional stories and analytic resources that may be helpful as you tackle these questions at www.bridgespan.org/givesmart.

What questions matter most to you?

Whatever those specifics may be, however, choosing to ignore these questions will reduce the probability of achieving results. Philanthropy almost always involves a fair degree of trial and error. By prioritizing thought as well as action—thinking through the relevant questions with appropriate rigor and discipline—you will reduce the frequency of your errors and make your trials more valuable. The good news is that even a modest amount of thought can help you avoid philanthropy's insidious traps and start you on a path toward better performance. The rewards of doing so will multiply over time, as communities are better served and society's thorniest issues are more effectively addressed.

There will be rewards for you personally, as well. Your legacy may help to establish standards of excellence, inspiring others to use their philanthropic resources more effectively in pursuit of their own ambitious aspirations. Your success at giving will provide an enhanced sense of meaning and fulfillment in your life—sentiments you will hear often in the voices of donors throughout these pages. And when you close your eyes at night, you will do so confident that you have accomplished as much with your philanthropy as you possibly could have.

I

WHAT ARE MY VALUES AND BELIEFS?

THIS IS A BOOK ABOUT PEOPLE, MONEY, and impact: generous people with money, the hard-working people who need that money, and the social impact that both groups hope to achieve. In short, it is a book about turning philanthropic resources into real-world results.

Great philanthropy is distinguished not by the sheer size of a gift or grant, but by what it accomplishes. As you will discover, it comes in an almost infinite variety of shapes and forms. What you choose to focus your philanthropy on is yours to decide. There is a world of exciting possibilities from which to choose, just as there are many good choices for actually structuring your philanthropy.

If you are truly intent on generating results, however, there are more (and less) successful ways to approach your

---

Unless otherwise noted, throughout this book we discuss philanthropic decision making through the lens of a specific gift, grant, or initiative (meaning a set of grants intended to contribute to the same overarching goal). We made this choice for the sake of narrative clarity, recognizing that, at any given time, most donors and foundations pursue a portfolio of philanthropic activities.

philanthropy. The approach presented here revolves around a series of disciplined decisions about what you intend to accomplish with a particular gift or grant (the real-world results that will define success for you). How you (and others) will go about achieving those results. And what you will do to help improve them over time. It also assumes that you will be willing to hold yourself accountable for achieving results on society's behalf.

For most individuals, a feeling of personal accountability is something that evolves over time, as their passion for an organization or a cause leads them to become ever more deeply involved. Depending on your circumstances, this approach may be relevant for some or all of your philanthropy. As a donor, you may find it applies to only a portion of your giving, whereas if you are a professional (a foundation chief executive, say, or a senior program officer), it might well be appropriate for most, if not all, of the work you do.

Why would you choose to adopt an approach centered squarely on delivering results? To us, the compelling answer is that it increases the opportunity to have a real impact on the issues or causes you are most passionate about. To illustrate, we'll look at three examples of generous individuals who have done, or are focused on doing, precisely that. As you will see, the roots of this approach reach back more than a century, and yet it is as contemporary as today's entrepreneurs-turned-philanthropists. First, though, we want to say a word about "you."

Although this chapter is framed primarily from the vantage point of donors, the question it poses and the issues it raises are relevant for every individual seriously engaged in philanthropy. Because philanthropy is an intensely personal pursuit, values and beliefs matter intensely—not just for the benefactors themselves, but also for the family members, trustees, and foundation leaders who work with or for them. These individuals may be strongly influenced by the wishes of a living donor, or informed by the intent of a now-deceased donor, but ultimately their decisions will be grounded in what they believe is right. This pattern is most clearly visible in the foundation world, where new chief executives (and program officers) routinely change priorities and develop new strategies, within the broad frameworks typically set by a donor's original intentions. So, whether philanthropy is (or becomes) a full-time occupation, or engages you for just a few hours a month, you are the "you" we are addressing, not only here but throughout this book.

THE OMIDYARS:
USING THE WEB TO DRIVE CHANGE

Pierre Omidyar, the founder of eBay, and his wife, Pam, belong to the current generation of philanthropists who are "giving while living." These new philanthropists often seek ways to bring their professional experience and business acumen to the pursuit of social good. A prime example is the Omidyars' support for Ushahidi, whose name comes from the word for "testimony" or "witness" in Swahili.

Ushahidi is a Web platform that gathers data from individual emails and text messages and represents it in a visual format (such as a map or timeline) that can inform others and galvanize them to act. First used in 2008 to chart post-election violence in Kenya, Ushahidi enables citizens to use their cell phones to report violent events and other incidents; these reports are then aggregated, highlighting where help is most needed. Using technology to harness the power of the individual, Ushahidi "crowdsources" crisis information from the people most directly involved, making it harder for those in power (legitimately or not) to suppress what is actually happening on the ground.[1]

Humanity United, founded by Pam Omidyar in 2005 to build peace and advance human freedom across the globe, was one of Ushahidi's earliest supporters. After the Kenyan election, Humanity United provided counsel and funding to the organization to launch a second iteration of is work.[2] Impressed by Ushahidi's success, Omidyar Network, another of the couple's philanthropies, supported the organization with a grant for further growth, funding both a physical hub in Kenya and efforts to scale.[3]

Since its original deployment in Kenya, the Web-based Ushahidi platform has been used by citizens and organizations around the world to publicize and spark real-time responses to other humanitarian crises, natural catastrophes, like the 2010 earthquake in Haiti, and environmental disasters, like the BP explosion in the Gulf of Mexico.

JULIUS ROSENWALD: BUILDING BETTER SCHOOLS

Julius Rosenwald, one of the guiding geniuses behind the creation of the Sears, Roebuck & Co. empire, decided at a relatively early age to devote his immense fortune to philanthropic ends. Described as "down-to-earth, flexible, compassionate, and people—rather than institution—centered," he was committed to "making American democracy work and to the struggle against racial and religious intolerance."[4]

Rosenwald began his philanthropy by making relatively small gifts. In 1912, for example, on the occasion of his fiftieth birthday, he donated $25,000 to help Booker T. Washington expand his Tuskegee Institute to smaller, far-flung campuses. When Washington found he couldn't use the final $2,100 of the grant for the stated purpose, he asked Rosenwald's permission to build six small rural schoolhouses in Alabama for African American children. Rosenwald agreed.

Based on positive initial results at those first six schools, Rosenwald gave Washington another $30,000. The immediate goal was to build a hundred similar schools across rural Alabama. But Rosenwald also hoped that these "Rosenwald schools" would spark "a revolution in public funding for education [by shaming] public officials into spending equal, even if separate, amounts for the education of black and white people."[5]

The highly visible program was considered a great success, and soon other Southern states asked Rosenwald to expand his program to include them. By 1920, the Julius Rosenwald Fund was managing a $500,000 annual school-building program. What followed was nothing less than the education revolution Rosenwald had envisioned. By 1928, one in five of all black schools in the South were Rosenwald schools, and one in three of the region's black students were being taught in those schools.

By the time of Rosenwald's death in 1932, when the fund was formally terminated, the program had helped build 4,977 rural schools. Significantly, the fund contributed only about

15 percent of the overall cost of those schools; the remainder came from state and local resources. Earlier than many philanthropists, Rosenwald recognized the "power of leverage" (although he probably didn't use that label, any more than he would have tried to analyze his "social return on investment"). Not only did communities help pay for their "black schools"; in many cases, the construction of a new and relatively well-equipped black school compelled local authorities to build an equally good school for their white students. Education was upgraded for black and white children across the South.[6]

JOHN DORR:
STRIPING THE NATION'S HIGHWAYS

Dr. John V. N. Dorr, a metallurgist, chemical engineer, and protégé of Thomas Edison, founded an engineering firm that made him wealthy enough to establish the Dorr Foundation in 1940. Created to support advances in the fields of chemistry and metallurgy, the foundation initially funded a wide range of small projects. Then Dorr's wife, Nell, made an observation about drivers that charted a whole new course for the foundation. She pointed out that after dark, especially in bad weather, headlight glare from oncoming traffic made drivers either hug the center line of the highway or swerve away from that line onto the soft shoulder of the road—sometimes with tragic consequences.[7]

Thinking about the problem his wife had identified, Dorr became convinced that painting a white stripe on the far right side of the road to demarcate the outside edge of the pavement would not only minimize the threat to drivers, but also make pedestrians safer. In 1953, his foundation began lobbying highway officials in Connecticut to test his theory on a stretch of the Merritt Parkway, a thirty-eight-mile scenic highway stretching from the New York border northeast to the Housatonic River, with the foundation underwriting the cost of the experiment. Results were positive, and soon the shoulders along the entire parkway were striped.

Impressed, officials in New York ran their own test on the Hutchinson River Parkway, which connected with the Merritt, and the results were equally compelling. In the seven months prior to striping, there were 102 accidents with a total of 49 injuries. In the seven months after striping, there were only 46 accidents with 27 injuries: a 55 percent reduction.

Long years of advocacy on the part of the Dorr Foundation ensued, with highway departments across the country, reluctant to spend the $150 per mile needed to stripe a shoulder, only grudgingly accepting the mounting evidence of its effectiveness. By the early 1960s, however, the highway shoulder line had gained near-universal acceptance and application across the country. As a result of the foundation's money and more than a decade of relentless lobbying on Dorr's part, an increasingly mobile population became a lot safer, and thousands upon thousands of lives were saved.

These three examples are different in many respects, including the values and beliefs that shaped the donors' choices; the scale, scope, and degree of difficulty of what they set out to do; and their approaches to creating change. What they have in common is the desire to use their philanthropic resources to make very specific differences in the world.

This may sound like the most common of common denominators. After all, you would be hard pressed to find a philanthropist who doesn't hope to make a difference, let alone one who would knowingly set out to waste hard-earned money. But people get involved in philanthropic activities for all sorts of reasons, and while the altruistic impulse to do "good" is almost always part of a decision to be generous, what exactly that "good" might be isn't always top of mind.

The point is simple: setting out to do "good" isn't enough. You will accomplish far more if you set out to accomplish something specific. The process of deciding what that might be begins with identifying what it is you're most passionate about and where you aspire to make a difference.

ALL PHILANTHROPY IS PERSONAL

Philanthropy is as individual as the universe of philanthropists is diverse, for the original benefactor and for the family members, trustees, and staff who may play a role (in parallel or subsequently) in giving it away.

Philanthropists can and do support almost anything, from educating school children, to saving the lives of drowsy motorists, to giving people the information they need to take action on their own behalf and on behalf of others who may be halfway around the world. This absolute freedom is philanthropy's great strength, in that it allows donors to express their individuality, creates room for innovation, and provides support for the myriad institutions and centers of power and activity that characterize democratic societies. But it can also become its Achilles' heel, when a donor's gifts are unconsidered or spread so thin that none of them ever amounts to very much.

A wealthy friend of ours realized he had fallen into just this trap when he told us that he had supported 167 organizations and causes in the course of the preceding year. (It was tax time, so the number was fresh in his mind when we had the conversation.) We asked him how many of them were causes to which he would have liked to commit his time and energy as well as his money. "Well," he replied, "you could count those on the fingers of one hand."

Moving beyond this kind of reflexive giving begins with clarifying your values and beliefs. One of the paradoxes of philanthropy is that, although it performs best when it is focused on results, almost every philanthropic initiative contains a huge dose of "me." As a result it is, and should be, substantively defined and shaped by the passions of the donor or, in the case of a foundation, its benefactor(s).

So, let's assume for the moment that you are a newly engaged donor, or a recently hired foundation president, committed to achieving social impact by exploring the kind of intentional approach we are proposing. You are looking at, literally, a world of good choices. How might you begin? A real-world example, although a somewhat extraordinary one, offers some clues.

Peter and Jennifer Buffett learned in the spring of 2006 that his father, legendary investor Warren Buffett, was going to transfer a huge sum, something upward of a billion dollars, into their family's NoVo Foundation. "You better get home, I think our life just changed," Peter told Jennifer after getting his father's fax. Though given no specific directives, they were encouraged to "focus the new funds and your energy on a relatively few activities in which NoVo can make an important difference."[8]

In response to this unique challenge, the Buffetts decided to embark on a joint journey of discovery. "We were in the office together every single day," Jennifer remembers. "We talked to so many people leading organizations to find out what was the 'opportunity of our time.' Little by little, trickles of information from hundreds of people around the world started to merge into patterns."[9]

One pattern, in particular, began to resonate with the Buffetts' own values and beliefs: the imbalance of power between men and women around the world. As Jennifer describes it, "In Africa or India you really see that men have the power and the dominant position, while women do not. And yet women are saddled with the burdens of holding families and communities together." These observations and experiences eventually led the Buffetts to focus the NoVo Foundation on "empowering women and girls as the primary agents of change."[10]

Having chosen an issue, they began by making significant grants to experienced, well-run organizations focused on the status of women and girls, such as Women for Women International and the International Rescue Committee. As they learned more about the field, the Buffetts increased their level of commitment even more. In May 2008, the NoVo and Nike foundations jointly announced a combined $100 million investment in the "Girl Effect," aimed at helping the 600 million adolescent girls in developing countries bring social and economic change to their families, communities, and countries.[11]

This investment has already begun to show results. For example, the Berhane Hewan initiative, located in a region of Ethiopia where 43 percent of girls are married by age fifteen, has helped 11,000 girls (97 percent of the participants) stay in school and delay marriage. Safe and Smart Savings has given 23,000 Kenyan girls access to savings accounts and financial education, thereby offering them a way to begin building an asset base and developing their economic independence. Through the Girl Effect, and other strategic initiatives focused on tragic problems like sex trafficking and violence against women in post-conflict environments, the Buffetts and NoVo are making gains on the issues about which they are most passionate.

No matter how well endowed your philanthropic activities are—even if you are fortunate enough to have a billion dollars in the bank!—the number of good things you *could* do will always be greater than the resources you can bring to bear (not just dollars, but also your time and influence). The level of need at home and throughout the world is enormous, even overwhelming. New, urgent, or exciting opportunities arise continuously. And, of course, once people discover that you are inclined to be generous, the flow of requests for help arriving on your doorstep will increase dramatically.

It is impossible to invest significantly in a great many things at once, however. This is the trap into which our friend (and a great many other philanthropists) regularly fall. It's not so much a question of making a "wrong" choice as it is of failing to make a choice in the first place. The temptation to do everything and satisfy everyone may generate accolades, but it rarely generates results.

WHAT DO YOU REALLY CARE ABOUT?

As you think about establishing your priorities in the midst of a world of good choices, there are several things to keep in mind. First, no one else can make these decisions for you. Someone else's passion can inspire you, and perhaps draw you in to work with them. But if you are really going to commit yourself—your expertise and energy, as well as your money—you have to clarify your philanthropic priorities, based on your values and beliefs. This principle applies whether you are the primary donor, a family member, or a foundation executive responsible for interpreting "donor intent."

Second, at this stage there are no inherently right choices. Your philanthropic priorities will be determined by the things you are passionate about and believe are worth doing. As you begin to reflect on what those things might be, you may find it helpful to think about some of the broad categories that have provided anchor points for others' efforts over the years: people, problems, places, pathways, and philosophies.

People. Like the Buffetts and Julius Rosenwald, you may be drawn to help a specific group of people address circumstances that are defining (and probably limiting) their lives. Consider Larry and Joyce Stupski, whose foundation seeks to "improve life options for children of color and poverty."[12]

Larry Stupski is the former president of the Charles Schwab Corporation; Joyce spent many years as a special-education teacher and administrator in the Chicago and San Francisco public schools before founding a successful management communications firm. Both of them believe firmly that education

What do you really care about?

is the most important factor in transforming the lives of disadvantaged children.

Since its launch in 1996, the Stupski Foundation has worked with more than thirty large urban school districts across the country, with an increasing emphasis on understanding what it takes to make change happen on the ground in classrooms and what is needed at the district and state level to foster and support that change. Through their work (and the work of others) in education, the Stupskis are striving to help disadvantaged children overcome the constraints of poverty and racial inequality.

Problem. John Dorr became obsessed with the problem of highway safety. For Steve Case and many other philanthropists, the problem that engages their passion is finding a cure for a deadly or debilitating disease.

In 2001, Dan Case, a prominent investment banker, was diagnosed with a brain tumor. Frustrated with the slow pace of medical research and the inability or unwillingness of researchers to share information, he and his brother Steve (the former chairman of AOL), along with their wives, Stacy and Jean, cofounded Accelerate Brain Cancer Cure (ABC^2)—a nonprofit with an entrepreneurial approach to funding research and speeding up the drug-discovery process. Dan died in 2002, but the research goes on.[13] Already, ABC^2 has invested $14 million in the therapeutic development pipeline and, with partners, has demonstrated the effectiveness of new treatments.

Place. Maintaining or restoring the health and vitality of a particular geography is a cause that has captivated many philanthropists. Dwayne Steele was a Kansas native who put down roots in Hawaii, where he built a highly successful construction business. An early friendship with a local musician inspired him to study Hawaiian. The language was on the brink of extinction, and, appalled by the thought of losing such a fundamental piece of the culture he had come to love, he embarked on a philanthropic quest to preserve it. With the help and support of local Hawaiians, he began publishing

Hawaiian-language textbooks to encourage more teaching. This led to a larger, ongoing effort to publish a wide range of materials, including dictionaries, storybooks, and oral histories as well as to digitize Hawaiian-language articles and newspapers dating back to the nineteenth century.

Steele also helped to fund the creation of several Hawaiian-language elementary schools. Initially developed to revive the language among younger generations of native islanders, these schools are now attracting "new" Hawaiians of every ethnicity and race. Although Steele passed away in 2006, Hawaiians and local philanthropists claim he initiated a "Hawaiian cultural renaissance" and credit him with not just the preservation of the language, but its rebirth.[14]

Dorothy Chandler, wife of the publisher of the *Los Angeles Times*, was also passionate about a place, in this case, downtown Los Angeles. Chandler believed that what kept Los Angeles from being recognized as a major world city was its lack of cultural facilities. Starting in the 1950s, she focused on building a permanent winter home for the LA Philharmonic, which could also provide a centerpiece for other cultural activities. Joining forces with studio head Lew Wasserman and others to bridge the city's notorious social and geographic divides, Chandler fund-raised for nearly a decade, once raising a then-unprecedented $400,000 at a single event. Her efforts culminated in 1964 with the opening of the three-theater Los Angeles Music Center in downtown LA, which now includes the Dorothy Chandler Pavilion, the longtime home of the Academy Awards. For her commitment to advancing the city, *Time* magazine put her on its cover in 1964, and today Los Angeles is widely recognized as a center of arts and culture.[15]

Pathway. A strongly held belief in the importance of a particular approach provides the foundation of many philanthropists' activities. Consider the Omidyars' belief in the power of technology and individuals to drive change, or Duncan Campbell's belief in the power of a mentor to guide and support youth.

Campbell, the child of alcoholic parents, grew up in Portland, Oregon, and remembers how important positive, stable adult figures were in his life as his family's circumstances spiraled downward.[16] In 1993, he founded Friends of the Children, which brings caring, consistent relationships with adults to at-risk youth facing challenges like his own, or worse. Campbell's support of mentoring as an effective pathway has proven itself: 85 percent of the young people in the program graduate from high school, versus the national average of around 70 percent; and 99 percent avoid becoming early parents themselves, even though at least 60 percent were born to teen parents.[17]

Philosophy. Lastly, your beliefs about how the world works, or should work, might be your anchor, as they are for George Soros. Soros, a global financier who helped invent the hedge fund, is founder and chairman of the Open Society Foundations, which seek to build "vibrant and tolerant democracies."[18] Soros defected from Hungary when the Soviet Union took over the country in 1946. He has spent many years and large sums of money personally doing battle against totalitarianism in novel ways within a wide range of contexts; for example, supplying photocopiers to Hungarian dissidents, giving funds to the Polish Solidarity movement, supporting educational radio programs in Mongolia, and contributing

$100 million to give every regional university in Russia access to the Internet. Today, the Open Society Foundations, formally organized in 1995, serves as the hub of a network of thirty-three foundations that operate in sixty countries worldwide, working through local advisors who, like Soros, are committed to promoting democracy.

Financier and former secretary of commerce Pete Peterson is another philanthropist inspired to take action by his deeply held beliefs; in his case, beliefs about the economic principles needed to drive a healthy society. Increasingly concerned about ballooning federal deficits, a mushrooming national debt, low national and personal savings rates, and other troubling economic trends, he invested $1 billion in the Peter G. Peterson Foundation, founded in July 2008 to raise public awareness about key economic and fiscal-policy issues. He also chose to focus many of his foundation's activities on reaching young people: in its first year of operation, for example, the foundation funded *I.O.U.S.A.*, a documentary film, and partnered with MTV to produce a campaign aimed at helping college students take control of their financial futures.[19]

By now you may have noticed that we haven't yet said anything about the role of data and analysis in deciding what your priorities will be. This silence is intentional. Data will be a great friend once you begin to frame a strategy for pursuing your philanthropy. But it isn't much help when you're getting started, because it can't tell you what you care most about. Whether it would be better to clean up the oceans, end human trafficking, right the U.S. economy, or do something else entirely is not a decision that lends itself to data-driven analysis.

The executive director of a foundation whose benefactor had built a strongly market-oriented and customer-driven high-tech business learned this lesson early in his tenure. The donor and his spouse were eager to "fix" public education in the United States, and they and the foundation's director were sure that the right data would identify the biggest problem facing underserved kids.

Before too long, they were awash in data, which documented myriad serious problems as well as all sorts of interesting options for action. None of it was any use, however, until the donors began to clarify which of the myriad players in the education space—students, teachers, principals, parents—they cared most about helping.

A PERSONAL JOURNEY OF DISCOVERY

As a donor, choosing your philanthropic priorities is a values-driven decision or, more accurately, a series of decisions that you will make not just once but many times. The act of making explicit choices is the first step of a personal journey of discovery that will likely last as long as you are actively engaged in your philanthropy.

People begin to clarify their values and beliefs in many different ways, and every individual needs to find his or her own path. In the late 1990s, Microsoft founder Bill Gates and his wife, Melinda, came across an article about rotavirus, a disease that was killing half a million children every year in the developing world. Recognizing that such a death toll would be seen as intolerable in any developed country, they realized that only one, terrible inference could be drawn: some lives are considered more valuable than others. Shortly thereafter, the Gateses established their foundation and published a letter explaining what had motivated them. Recounting that experience in a 2007 speech, Melinda Gates said:

> We knew what we stood for: that all lives have equal value— that starving children in African and Indian slums are just as precious as your children or mine, that families struggling in American inner cities matter just as much as families in safe, suburban neighborhoods. Ultimately, all people, no matter where they live, deserve a chance to live a healthy, productive life.[20]

As you get started on your own journey, you may find that there are several things you care deeply about (or, if you are a foundation executive, that your donor's intent is broad and vague). At this stage that's not a problem, because you're simply identifying what you will (and won't) try to learn more about in the near future. When the time comes to develop a strategy for pursuing your goals, your "will not pursue" list will become as important as your priorities. But that time decidedly is not now.

Take the time to learn and to expand your horizons. Talk with your spouse and family. Go on an extended retreat. Bounce ideas off mentors, colleagues, and advisors—the wise men and women in your life. Read (a lot). Visit nonprofit organizations whose work other people admire. Listen to other engaged philanthropists talk about what they do. Capture your thoughts and revisit them. One philanthropist we know began his philanthropic journey by scribbling down three words: "youth," "learning," and "community." Revisited and tested over time, those same three words have now informed and guided more than twenty years of successful philanthropic efforts.

CLARITY IS CRITICAL

If you move to strategy too quickly, before you've appropriately clarified your values and beliefs, you are likely to waste resources jumping from one area of focus to another while you sort things out in real time. You can also do damage, not only to your own reputation but also to your grantees. As we will underscore in later chapters, the donor-grantee relationship is both critically important and easily abused. As a philanthropist, you have a positive obligation not only to do good but also, insofar as possible, to do no harm. Clarifying your values and beliefs before you establish your priorities helps you achieve both ends.

Clarity is especially important with giving that focuses on complex problems. When you contribute to the construction of sanitary facilities in Guatemala or the wing of a research laboratory, you are addressing a specific challenge that is both concrete (literally) and bounded. The odds that you will lose faith or change direction in midstream are relatively small. This is not necessarily the case with many of the other issues that philanthropy addresses, like improving the well-being of disadvantaged children in rural communities or helping ex-offenders leave prison behind them for good.

Social issues like these are complex, with many contributing factors. Results often take a long time to emerge, and it can be years before consequences are visible. A decision to get involved will require persistence, commitment, a willingness to stay the course, and an acceptance of a certain amount of ambiguity. It may never be possible to draw a clear line between your contributions and whatever outcomes are successfully achieved. In such situations, clarity about your values—why you became engaged in the first place—can provide a strong incentive to stay the course.

Clarifying your values is also the best way we know to ensure that your philanthropy will continue to express what matters most to you. The specific priorities you establish today may evolve and change over the course of time. But deep personal values tend to persist and, as a result, they can provide a continuing touchstone throughout a lifetime of philanthropy. If you establish a foundation intended to last in perpetuity, explicitly clarifying your values will make it far more likely that your foundation will continue to embody and act on them long after you've left the stage.

The early history of the John D. and Catherine T. Mac-Arthur Foundation, one of the largest in the United States, provides a cautionary example of what can happen when a donor isn't explicit about his or her intentions. When John MacArthur set up the foundation in 1978, he established a small board composed of his wife and son, Roderick; the radio commentator Paul Harvey, whose show his company had sponsored; and three business associates. He purposely gave the board no instruction about how the foundation should be organized or what it should do. "I know of a number of foundations where the donors tried to run them from their graves," he explained. "I have guaranteed the trustees that when I am gone, they can run the show."[21]

MacArthur died just as his foundation was beginning its

work, and the trustees did indeed run the show, though not in the ways he might have imagined. Almost immediately, a dispute erupted over the direction the foundation should take (and also over how to accomplish the legally mandated diversification of the foundation's assets). On one side were MacArthur's former associates, self-described "Midwestern businessmen devoted to free enterprise and opposed to more government controls." On the other, MacArthur's son, who "declared that foundations had to be on the cutting edge of social change, that they should lead government 'as its social conscience,' and that he would like to see the MacArthur Foundation concentrate heavily on funding 'maverick geniuses' to pursue their own ideas and make their own discoveries.'"[22] Just about the only thing they could agree on was that the trustees should play the lead role in directing the foundation's activities and affairs.

The following year, the board voted to enlarge itself to fifteen members (including a Nobel Prize–winning scientist and the president emeritus of MIT) to help resolve the directional disputes. Although individual trustees initiated some excellent programs, including the MacArthur Fellows Program, which is probably still its best known initiative, the wrangling continued. It broke into active warfare when Roderick brought suit (later dropped) against all but two members of the board, charging them with squandering the foundation's assets and enriching themselves. Roderick's death at the end of 1984 quieted the tumult, but it would take another fifteen years before problems with the foundation's direction were entirely resolved.[23]

In sum, being clear yourself is what makes it possible for others to work effectively with you, and for you to work effectively with others. This is crucially important because, although the decisions may be yours to make, you are seldom alone in making them. Even if all the money behind the effort is yours, others will step forward and exert an influence. The more articulate you are about your values, the more likely it is that your values will exert the appropriate influence.

AMBIGUITY IS THE ENEMY

On the evening of January 19, 1955, CBS aired the first installment of a television drama called *The Millionaire*. The show centered on a semiretired industrialist named John Beresford Tipton, who anonymously bestowed million-dollar gifts (that's $8 million, in current dollars) on seemingly random and always unsuspecting individuals. To the viewing audience, Tipton (obscured by a high-backed leather executive chair) remained only a raspy voice and besuited right arm: a shadowy figure who handed over a cashier's check to his executive secretary, Michael Anthony, for delivery to that week's recipient. John Beresford Tipton seems to have acted entirely alone. There were no family members, no trustees, and no staff other than Michael Anthony involved in his philanthropy. Nor did he have either repeat grantees or any ongoing relationships with the objects of his generosity.

This is *not* the way philanthropy works in the real world. As a real-world philanthropist, you almost certainly will have others around you. You may have a spouse, or family members, or interested friends, or professional advisors, or all of the above. If you've created a foundation, you have trustees and probably at least a few staff members. If you are the leader of a large foundation, it's likely that you have a significant staff to manage—each with his or her own set of values, beliefs, and related opinions that may or may not be well synchronized with the benefactor's or your own.

All these people have their own ideas about what is worth doing, and why. Being clear about your values will make it much easier to achieve alignment. It will force differences of opinion to the surface, and perhaps head off trouble down the road.

In the trust indenture creating the Duke Endowment, which benefits Duke University and several other educational institutions, as well as communities in North and South Carolina, tobacco magnate James Buchanan Duke required that the entire endowment document be read aloud annually at a trustees' meeting. He believed that the document captured his intentions, what *he* valued, and he wanted it to continue to shape the trustees' deliberations and decisions indefinitely.[24]

Unfortunately, achieving this kind of clarity doesn't always come easily or naturally. Human nature often encourages us to avoid confrontation, especially with family members and close friends. Surfacing your personal beliefs and then talking about them with others can be a messy, emotional, tiring process, one that's likely to be imperfect, at best. This is a discomfort well worth bearing, however, because the costs of ambiguity on this front can be extremely high.

Consider what happened to a philanthropist we know, whom we'll call Chester. Like most of us, Chester has definite views about public policy and political preferences that reflect his values, beliefs, and worldview. Unfortunately, he did not realize the link between his political orientation and his philanthropic values until much too late in the day.

Chester first funded his family foundation over a decade ago, when he was still working long hours in business. As the foundation grew, Chester recruited a former employee, Alan, to serve as president. At first, Alan worked directly with Chester, helping him respond to charitable requests, coordinate trustee meetings, and manage existing grants. However, Chester's corporate responsibilities were incredibly time consuming, and, without explicitly thinking about it, he gradually delegated more and more authority to Alan, while simultaneously further empowering his family-dominated board. Because of scheduling conflicts, he was sometimes unable to attend board meetings, and he rarely read all the details embedded in the hefty board books.

Alan, meanwhile, designed high-level program strategies, which the board endorsed, for the foundation's priority areas: public health, education, and the environment. He hired a team, and they worked hard to bring exciting funding requests to the trustees. Over time, the foundation dramatically increased its annual giving, and Alan clearly came into his own as president.

Then, rather abruptly, Chester retired. He was burned out and had decided to devote his remaining years to philanthropy and service. He hoped to leverage his foundation's work by applying his energetic hands-on approach to its grant making, and infusing his deeply held conservative beliefs into everything his foundation did. Exerting a positive influence on public policy would be his philanthropic legacy.

There was, however, a little problem: neither Alan nor the staff shared Chester's values and politics. They were more liberal, as were two of Chester's three children (all trustees), a situation he had largely chosen to ignore. His family foundation, now fully funded with his hard-earned money, had apparently taken on a life of its own.

Chester faced a Hobson's choice: accept the status quo and thus forfeit his desired future; or fire everyone and endure the collateral damage to his family, his reputation, and his foundation. By not confronting the central question of how his values and beliefs should be reflected in his philanthropy, Chester had created a serious problem for both himself and many others.

We said earlier that being clear about your own values is what makes it possible for others to work effectively with you. Here we are making the flip side of that same argument: ambiguity makes it harder for others to work effectively with and for you. Ambiguity will make it harder to make key strategic decisions downstream: identifying a real opportunity, as opposed to a diversion, for instance, or selecting the right grantees.

These problems will only compound as time goes on, especially in the absence of a living donor. Based on our observations, what happens next is highly predictable: Adrift in ambiguity, decision makers "split the difference." Less and less money goes to more and more recipients. Processes (such as the grant-making cycle) take on a life of their own. The result, in most cases, might be summed up in the phrase "satisfactory underperformance." Things are still getting done, but without as much impact as would otherwise be the case. And while everyone involved may be feeling good about what they're doing, that does not necessarily mean they're actually doing good.

In contrast, clarity enables others to honor your intent, while simultaneously responding to the needs of their own time. The Alfred P. Sloan Foundation offers a fine example. The foundation has long had a focus on promoting public understanding of science. Did Sloan, the guiding genius behind General Motors, contemplate the possibility that his foundation might one day be helping to produce plays dealing with scientific topics? Perhaps not. And yet, more than a dozen plays (including the acclaimed dramas *Copenhagen* by Michael Frayn and *Proof* by David Auburn) have been staged with help from the Sloan Foundation. Alfred Sloan, we think, would be quite pleased.

PHILANTHROPY IS NOT A ONE-TIME EVENT

We've introduced the idea that wrestling with your philanthropic aspirations isn't a one-time event. Nor, as the Sloan example illustrates, is it a question relevant only to living donors. Any number of triggers might persuade you, or your heirs and trustees, or your foundation staff, to revisit the question of priorities.

For example, your personal perspective may change over time, as your experiences accumulate and your interests evolve. At age thirty-nine you may want to serve poor children; at age fifty-nine you may want to build organizational capacity to combat AIDS in Africa; and at age seventy-nine you may want to sustain both these efforts through advocacy. Or a change in financial circumstances (in either direction) may force hard choices and new decisions. The recession of 2008 dramatically reduced the resources of many philanthropists and mandated reevaluation of their priorities. In contrast, the Buffetts had the happier challenge of responding to an even more impressive surge in the assets of their foundation.

Over time, the people engaged in your philanthropy are also likely to change. Your children will become old enough to participate in your family foundation, or your foundation will bring on new leadership. New participants will ask new questions, pushing back on existing priorities. Or the issues you care about may change based on new solutions or new attention from government or other nonprofits. Context constantly evolves. Maybe the problems you've tackled will be solved. After all, even polio was cured!

Regardless of the specifics, you should expect that at some point events may make you or the decision makers in your foundation step back and reconsider. If you are clear enough about your aspirations, values, and beliefs, the new priorities that emerge will continue to reflect the good you most want to see done in the world.

2

WHAT IS "SUCCESS" AND HOW CAN IT BE ACHIEVED?

NCE YOU'VE REFLECTED ON YOUR values and beliefs, and decided where you want to anchor your philanthropy, you're ready to start thinking about how you'll use your resources to best effect. In short, you're ready to get strategic. That doesn't mean abandoning what you're passionate about. It does mean bringing rigorous thinking and evidence into the decision-making mix.

Developing a strategy for your philanthropy is an iterative process that requires asking, and answering, three separate but related questions: "What will constitute success for this initiative?" "What will it take to achieve success?" and "What am I accountable for?" We find it helpful to think of this process as getting clear, getting real, and getting personal.

Getting clear involves defining success in terms specific enough to help you decide where to invest your resources.

Whatever your ultimate definition is, it should make it possible for you to determine what is in—and out of—bounds for a given initiative. *Getting real* involves laying out the sequence of activities or events that in your considered judgment are necessary to achieve success. (Philanthropists often refer to this as a "theory of change.") Finally, *getting personal* involves deciding whether you'll be willing and able to hold yourself accountable for success. Do you, in your own right or in collaboration with others, have the financial and nonfinancial resources to make pursuing the strategy you're envisioning plausible?

For simplicity, we'll explore the first two parts of the strategy process, getting clear and getting real, in this chapter. We'll pick up the third, which requires you to wrestle with the question of personal accountability for your philanthropy, in chapter three. In practice, however, the process is seldom this linear. What you want to achieve, how that might be accomplished, and the level of resources (financial and nonfinancial) required to be successful are pieces that ultimately have to form a coherent whole. So don't be surprised if you find that you have to cycle back and forth a few times— between your definition of success and your theory of change, and between those choices and the resources you can actually commit—in order to develop a strategy both ambitious enough to be inspiring and feasible enough to give you a real shot at achieving it.[1]

To see how these three pieces come together to create a robust strategy, consider how the senior decision makers at California's James Irvine Foundation developed the initiative that has come to be called "Linked Learning."

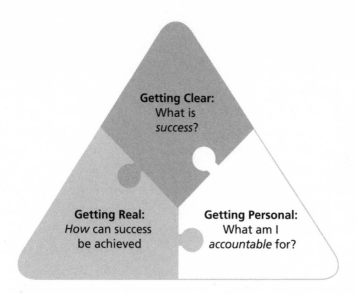

THE JAMES IRVINE FOUNDATION: LINKING HIGH SCHOOL TO COLLEGE AND CAREER

Established in 1937 by California agricultural pioneer James Irvine, the foundation's mission is to "expand opportunity for the people of California to participate in a vibrant, successful, and inclusive society."[2] To this end, the foundation's grant making focuses primarily on the arts, the state's public policy decision-making processes ("California democracy"), and youth (aged fourteen to twenty-four). The youth program's goal is "to increase the number of low-income youth in California who complete high school on time and attain a post-secondary credential [including two- and four-year degrees, post-secondary certification, or apprenticeship programs] by the age of 25."[3] Its cornerstone is a long-term initiative, begun in 2005, that links high school education to student interests and college and career preparation.

Propelling the initiative were some harsh realities. One-third of California's high school students drop out before graduation,[4] thereby becoming eight times more likely to be incarcerated than peers who make it through, and twice as likely to fall into poverty.[5] Another third of the state's young people graduate unprepared for post-secondary education,[6] yet three-quarters of the state's jobs require some education and training beyond high school.[7] The burden of these failures is heavy, for the young people who bear the costs directly and for their fellow Californians who confront them in the form of incarceration rates, public assistance needs, foregone tax revenues, health outcomes, and an inadequate supply of skilled labor.

The Irvine Foundation's leadership had already engaged in a three-year research and development phase, which included funding a variety of approaches to youth development and education, by the time they began to zero in on Linked Learning (formerly known in California as the "multiple pathways" approach). They had also studied the best thinking in the field and been struck by strong data showing that when students understand the connection between what they are learning and their future prospects, it leads to higher graduation rates, increased college enrollment, and higher earning potential.[8] With its student-centered emphasis, the Linked Learning approach also resonated strongly with core foundation values.

Ensuring that college-preparatory, career-themed pathways would be available to high school students throughout California (particularly those who come from low-income families) is no small challenge, however. Effective Linked Learning pathways integrate demanding technical education and real-world experience in professional fields like biomedicine, arts and media, and engineering with rigorous academics required for success in further education. But the quality of existing programs was mixed at best, and remedying that was only one of the hurdles that would have to be overcome. Among the others were providing learning communities for district and school leaders and coaching and professional development for teachers; curriculum development and technical assistance for schools introducing or upgrading programs; enacting new policies to enable key changes in school practices and procedures; mobilizing public support for Linked Leaning; and creating alliances with educators, businesspeople, parents, and students.

To meet these challenges, Irvine's leaders laid out a strategy with three parallel streams of activity: demonstrating what is possible, first at the level of individual schools and then at the district level (practice); creating interest in and reinforcing the growing momentum for these programs among parents, the business community, and community leaders (public will); and working with policy makers and educational leaders to secure funding and wider provision of services (policy).

To play a galvanizing role in this work, in 2006 they established ConnectEd: The California Center for College and Career, an independent nonprofit based in Berkeley with a staff of twenty. In addition to providing training and coaching, fostering collaboration, and serving as a hub to help build knowledge and awareness, ConnectEd has helped build a coalition of more than 180 organizations from education, industry, and labor to join in promoting the approach statewide.

Although the initiative is still in its early days, the results are encouraging. The schools initially included in the demonstration project had higher attendance and graduation rates than the state average, and six of the sixteen had graduation rates of 100 percent. Students throughout the network were also prepared for college, and in four of the schools a remarkable 90 percent of seniors met the criteria for admission to the University of California and California State University systems.[9] An evaluation of the work at the district level is now getting under way. Based on that evaluation, the Irvine Foundation will continue to refine its strategy to achieve more and better results. At the same time, its leadership is also continuing to explore and learn: in 2010 they began work to understand what it will take to extend the benefits of Linked Learning to out-of-school youth between the ages of eighteen and twenty-four.[10]

GETTING CLEAR: WHAT IS SUCCESS?

Broadly stated, a win in philanthropy is a win for society, a change for the better that probably wouldn't have occurred without a concerted effort to bring it about. Maybe that's a polluted river brought back to life, or lower maternal mortality rates in a developing country, or a sharp increase in the number of a city's chronically homeless men and women placed in permanent housing.

Getting clear about what will constitute success for a given grant or initiative involves translating the win you envision for society into some real-world result or outcome (like the ones described above) that can inform decisions about how and where to allocate precious resources most effectively. The broader the win you envision, the more important it will be to develop some real specificity about what it is you intend to accomplish with your piece of the puzzle.

For example, suppose that climate change is the issue you feel passionate about. You (like us) may have heard philanthropists wax eloquent about their determination to "reverse global warming." Such a vision can be inspirational and highly motivating. But besides being too big for any single nation-state— let alone any individual donor or foundation—to achieve, it is also too broad to help you make trade-offs. As a result, it cannot provide a useful lens for making decisions about how to allocate scarce philanthropic resources most effectively.

To develop that kind of strategic clarity, you need to translate your vision of a world in which global climate change has been reversed into specific high-level outcomes that can drive resource-allocation decisions and trade-offs. What might qualify? The passage of federal cap-and-trade legislation in the United States. Ten thousand acres of Brazilian rain forest saved from logging. A reduction in carbon emissions from coal-fired power plants in China.

Any one of these answers (along with many others we could have cited) represents an outcome that might contribute to the overarching goal of reversing climate change, as well as a definition of success that can serve to guide decision making. Which of them would be right for you (were this your passion) would ultimately depend on your beliefs and knowledge about how climate change can best be addressed, as well as on the resources you're able to bring to bear.

Getting to the right level of specificity requires the discipline to make explicit choices and trade-offs about whom you'll seek to serve or the issues you'll try to address. For example, one of the most basic trade-offs is whether to ease current suffering or work to address its root cause: providing regular support for a regional food bank, say, as against funding a training program designed to provide low-income individuals with a trade that can lead to a secure living-wage job. Both are fine options. Which one you sign up for and where you say no will be a function of your values and beliefs.

To illustrate the kinds of choices and degree of specificity required to reach a workable definition of success, let's look at a situation we've encountered on numerous occasions.

Many philanthropists are committed to reducing the number of disadvantaged youth in their communities. On the face of it, this definition of success sounds clear enough: you could count the number of such young people before and after your philanthropic intervention, and if the number dropped that would be a success. In practice, though, this definition raises many more questions than it answers.

For example, how would you define "disadvantaged"? Financially, socially, physically, or emotionally disadvantaged? Being a high school dropout? Growing up in a single-parent household? Having one parent, or even both parents, incarcerated? Being hungry, or obese? One or more of the above? Similarly, what do you mean by "youth"? Kids in preschool? Elementary or middle school children? High school students? Young adults? A group that spans several of these age ranges? And the questions go on from there: Which of the many problems your chosen group may be facing is the most important to address? How big a geographic area can you take

on, on your own or in collaboration with others? One neighborhood? A couple of neighborhoods? An entire school district? The entire city?

There is no easy way to make choices like these. You need
to consider "soft" values and "hard" evidence and data: both
what you care about, and what's already known about the relevant issues, including their size, severity, the basic causes,
and the potential solutions. Being explicit about the need to
make these choices and then having the discipline to make
them are prerequisites to giving smart.

Often, the presence of a strong nonprofit or nongovernmental organization (NGO) doing effective work in the area
you care most about can help you zero in on what will be
right for you. Consider the experience of Clarence Day, a Ten-
nessee entrepreneur who built his family's landholdings in
Mississippi into a major business conglomerate.[11]

Clarence Day: Serving Neglected Kids

Like the philanthropists in our hypothetical example, Day
had become deeply concerned about the kids at risk of failure
in his community. He had heard about Youth Villages, a
Memphis-based nonprofit founded in 1986. It had a national
reputation for working with children and families at highest
risk, helping them to live together successfully.[12] In 1999,
he called on its CEO, Patrick Lawler, and asked him to talk
to him about the kids that no one else wanted to help.[13]

Lawler responded by telling him about the problems of
older teenagers who were aging out of state-run foster care
programs. These were adolescents who typically bounced
from one foster care placement or group home to another
throughout their teen years. They often had significantly

lower levels of education than their peers, as well as a history of complex mental health issues and higher rates of substance abuse, criminal involvement, and teenage pregnancy. Equally important, they lacked support systems to help them make the difficult transition to adulthood. In too many cases, these disadvantaged young people, ill prepared to live adult lives, simply slipped through the cracks, ending up homeless, incarcerated, or dead before their time.

In 1999, the Day Foundation made a $2 million grant to fund the Youth Villages Transitional Living program. Its purpose was to help young people, aged seventeen to twenty-two, get a good start on adulthood by providing critical supports for housing, employment, and education.[14] The program delivered outstanding, consistent outcomes to a very hard-to-serve population. Whereas national studies estimate that over one-third of youth who age out of state custody will experience homelessness after leaving care, two years out of Transitional Living, 87 percent of the participants live in a homelike environment. And while typically only 55 percent of these at-risk youth avoid trouble with the law after care, 74 percent of those in Transitional Living have had no trouble with the law even two years after leaving the program.[15] Day and his foundation continued to support the program in Tennessee, including making a challenge grant to the governor to cofund an expansion to serve more youth. He also helped Youth Villages expand the program to other states. To date, Day's funding has supported more than three thousand youth in this program.[16]

A good working definition of success satisfies three important criteria. First, it reflects the values and beliefs of the philanthropist—directly, if he or she is making the decisions, and indirectly, if (as is the case in foundations) they are being made by others or are part of the legacy handed down from the founding donor to the current generation of decision makers. Second, it is specific enough to guide decisions about what you will and will not fund; you can actually use it to make trade-offs and develop a feasible strategy. Third, it will allow you to gauge progress, or the absence thereof. Over time, as the results of the work you are funding become known, you'll be able to judge whether things are moving in the right direction, or whether you need to recalibrate and correct course.

Clarence Day's definition of success met these criteria. So does the way that the Sandler Foundation defines success for ProPublica, the independent newsroom it founded and funds.

The Sandler Foundation:
Exposing Corruption and Abuses of Power

Herb and Marion Sandler made Golden West Financial Corporation one of the largest and most admired savings and loan companies in the country. Together they head up the Sandler Foundation, which has a broad portfolio of philanthropic interests including research on neglected diseases, advocacy on behalf of vulnerable peoples and environments, rebuilding the progressive infrastructure of the United States, and exposing corruption and abuses of power. ProPublica, the foundation's most recent philanthropic start-up, falls into this last category. "We cannot stand the abuse of power, or powerful people taking advantage of those who are less powerful, and we cannot stand corruption," Herb Sandler explains. "It's something that drives us crazy." Driven by this belief, the couple wanted to use a portion of their philanthropy to find and expose "the next Enron," and presumably head off future Enrons.[17]

At the same time, the Sandlers knew that, largely because of financial pressures, mainstream media were cutting back on investigative reporting, a resource-intensive activity and one of the key tools used to fight corruption. "We all know the potential for corruption in city government, state government, federal government, and major corporations, and somebody's got to be watching," Sandler says. "That's the muckraker tradition." With this tradition in mind, the Sandlers decided to launch and fund ProPublica, an "independent newsroom," to conduct in-depth investigative reporting and offer its output free of charge to mainstream news outlets such as the *New York Times*, *Washington Post*, and National Public Radio, to mention just a few of its partners.[18]

In line with the Sandlers' ultimate goal, as well as their values and beliefs, ProPublica's success is measured not by its output—the quality and number of stories picked up by mainstream media—but by outcomes: the impact of those stories. "As much as we admire investigative journalism, the story is not the end," Herb Sandler says. "If it doesn't have an impact, if it doesn't change the practice, it was an interesting exercise, but essentially meaningless."

This lens explains why, when the Sandlers are asked about ProPublica's successes, what they mention is not the Pulitzer Prize their organization shared with the *New York Times*. Instead, they'll talk about an article published in conjunction with the *Los Angeles Times*. The article, based on an investigation conducted by ProPublica, reported on the dysfunctional disciplinary procedures for California's licensed nurses. When nurses were accused of patient abuse or other misconduct, it took the California Board of Nursing an average of three years and five months to investigate and conclude complaints. During that time, the nurses were often allowed to continue practicing. When the story broke, Governor Arnold Schwarzenegger immediately stepped in and replaced most of the board's members—a direct response to the investigation's findings.[19]

GETTING REAL:
HOW CAN SUCCESS BE ACHIEVED?

Based on what you already know, you probably have some ideas about how the success you are beginning to envision might be realized. Now you need to figure out whether those ideas constitute a feasible strategy, or whether they are merely wishful thinking.

One way to do this is to articulate what many in the nonprofit sector refer to as a "theory of change." Put simply, a theory of change starts with the change in the world you want to see and works backward to lay out everything you think will need to happen to bring it about. It identifies the key players (including yourself) who will need to be involved, what each of those players will have to do, and why they are likely to behave in the way you expect. To bring this concept to life, let's look at a few real-world examples.

The Draper Richards Foundation:
Investing in Social Entrepreneurs

Silicon Valley venture capitalists William Draper and Robin Richards Donohoe established the Draper Richards

WHAT IS "STRATEGY"?

The aim of strategy in business is winning: relentlessly outcompeting competitors in the quest for customers, in order to generate the financial returns that propel shareholder value.

The aim of strategy in philanthropy is fundamentally different: instead of revolving around competition to earn profits, it revolves around collaboration to achieve social impact. For a donor trying to determine how to change the world for the better, popular business concepts like competitive strategy, business definition, and customer loyalty may not always be applicable.

Where philanthropy and business do overlap is in the idea that the essence of strategy, be it collaborative or competitive, is resource allocation. The more effective your resource allocation, the more likely you are to achieve the results you really want.

Disciplined and thoughtful resource allocation does not happen automatically. So it helps donors to have some guidance from concepts customized to social sector dynamics. "Theory of change" is one such concept. It attempts to define a successful outcome for a certain population (or problem), then describes the most important cause-and-effect actions required to create that success. "Theory of action" is a related concept that specifies the role an individual donor or foundation will play within a given landscape of other participants. A "logic model" is different still. It describes the inputs, outputs, and success of a specific programmatic approach to effecting change. It is easy for philanthropists, even those with substantial experience, to feel tortured by jargon and bewildered by the array of strategic approaches. Our advice is to keep it as simple as the circumstances allow.

Outstanding strategies do have a few proven hallmarks: build on your core strengths, maintain an external orientation, rigorously pursue facts, measure the few things that matter most, and never ever become complacent.

Foundation in 2002. Thanks to their professional experiences, they believe strongly in the value of backing competent and motivated individuals who can build businesses if they are given adequate seed money and guidance. When they set up their foundation, they carried this worldview into their philanthropic activities.[20]

"We believe that dedicated, talented leadership is the essence of social change," they wrote in describing their Social Entrepreneurs program. "To this end, we provide funding and business mentoring to social entrepreneurs as they begin their nonprofit organization." A similar theory of change, they explained, lay behind their Fellowship program: "By delivering support at the critical start-up phase, Draper Richards Fellowships help outstanding people create wide-ranging social change."

If change grows out of talented, energetic, dedicated leadership, then the philanthropist's role (as Draper and Donohoe see it) is to find and back those leaders. In addition, grantees must have an idea that's a potential game changer, a program that is showing evidence of effectiveness, and an operation that can be scaled.

Recognizing that these characteristics are as rare as they are essential, the foundation does not limit its grants to specific program areas. Instead, they are open to working with social entrepreneurs who are tackling a wide range of issues. Improving crop yields in Africa; helping wounded and disabled veterans become employable by placing them in service leadership positions across the United States; and providing low-income families in Pakistan with affordable access to quality catastrophic health care are among the goals their grantees pursue.

Draper Richards demands a comprehensive business plan from its potential grantees, and if and when that plan is accepted (after the foundation does its due diligence), the foundation and the grantee enter into a multiyear contractual relationship, with continued funding contingent on the grantee's meeting mutually agreed upon milestones. Throughout that relationship, Draper Richards offers strategic coaching and guidance, and seeks to immerse the social entrepreneurs in a "community of practice" so that they can learn from and help one another.

Draper Richards' definition of success is "outstanding people creating wide-reaching social change." While they do not expect every grantee to thrive, the foundation has racked up an impressive list of success stories. One of its earliest fellows, for instance, was John Wood, the founder of Room to Read, which builds schools and bilingual libraries to provide underprivileged children in the developing world with a chance to be educated. In the ten years since its founding (and the eight years since its Draper Richards grant in 2002), Room to Read has served more than 1.7 million children through its 440 schools, 5,100 libraries, and 4,000 scholarships for girls.

"You can't start a fire without a spark," says the Draper Richards Web site, quoting Bruce Springsteen. The spark, in the Draper Richards theory of change, is the effective leader who can light a particularly powerful fire if he or she has the right kinds of guidance and resources.

The Barbara Lee Family Foundation: Putting More Women in Public Office

The Barbara Lee Family Foundation offers an example of how being disciplined about where you choose to play within a larger theory of change can translate an expansive aspiration into a bounded, realistic strategy. Established in 1999, the foundation seeks to advance "women's equality and representation in American politics and in the field of contemporary art."[21] With $1.3 million in assets, the foundation's small staff is careful to pursue these broad interests deliberately and thoughtfully.

For example, the Women in Politics initiative springs from Lee's core belief that women's voices strengthen our democracy and enrich our culture. The program's goal, accordingly, is "engaging women fully in the American democratic process and promoting their participation at all levels of government." To achieve this goal, the foundation has a concise and simple, but far-ranging theory of change: help women get elected.

With limited resources, and an almost unlimited number of options for employing them within this theory of change, Lee and the foundation's staff have thought long and hard about exactly where they can best contribute. Because governors are effectively the CEOs of their states and the position has been a pipeline to the presidency, the foundation has funded nonpartisan research to better understand the barriers and challenges facing women seeking governorships, as well as to create strategies to combat them. In 2001, they began publishing resources in the form of guidebooks (sized to fit in a woman's purse) that are used by candidates, their campaign strategists and staff, and the wider public. According to foundation director Adrienne Kimmell, women across the country running for elective positions, ranging from on the school board to the governorship, credit the guides with "informing their strategies and helping them avoid falling into traps that have undone other women's candidacies."[22]

While Lee recognizes that the foundation will never be able to link successful campaigns directly (let alone exclusively) to its efforts, the number of female governors has more than doubled (from sixteen to thirty-four) in the past ten years. By all indications, Lee's relentless and highly focused efforts have been an important (albeit small) driver of this success.

A Generous Donor: Growing the Pie for Conservation

One New England philanthropist we know, who often prefers to remain anonymous in his giving, has a long history of supporting land conservation. Over time, however, his views on how best to go about doing that have changed, as he has become more engaged and more knowledgeable about the opportunities in and obstacles to preservation.

Our friend has always valued the nation's natural resources. "My parents were children of the Depression, and we did things as a family—like hiking and staying at state and national parks—that didn't cost a lot of money, because the money needed to be saved for education, or retirement, or the next Depression. Growing up in the New York City suburbs, I developed a real sort of astonished wonder at the fact that there were natural spaces people could enjoy for free."[23]

Guided by the belief that everyone should be able to enjoy nature, his definition of success is to conserve and protect land so that it will be available for future generations. To this end, his first theory of change was simple: he made personal contributions to conserve specific pieces of land, and, in his own words, "It felt pretty good." As he learned more about the challenges facing preserved land, however, his perspective shifted.

"I learned that the aggregate dollars spent on development are over twenty times those spent on preservation. Twenty times!" he recalls. "And if you step back, you realize we have a problem. If I have only one-twentieth as many dollars, I'd better be really, really strategic about where I put those dollars." With those numbers in mind, he decided that instead of just buying land himself, he would give money in ways that encouraged others to spend their dollars to protect land also. In this way, he could "grow the pie" for conservation.

Around this time, he attended a presentation on the results of the Pew Charitable Trust's challenge grants; the approach intrigued him, especially since the economic downturn had reduced giving to conservation. So he began issuing his own anonymous financial "challenges" to individual towns. If a town's voters would pass a referendum to tax themselves by issuing bonds to cover some of the cost of protecting their own vital natural resources, he would provide the necessary additional funds through a community foundation.

The first town to take up the challenge was Scarborough, Maine, which approved a $1 million bond referendum for conservation, earning another $200,000 from the philanthropist. More towns followed and, to date, only one community has turned down the option of taking on a challenge grant.[24]

As the challenge grants unfolded, the philanthropist realized he was seeing an even more important result: when citizens assume responsibility for conservation in their communities, they become what he calls "great defenders" of nature. He was leveraging his dollars, but he was also creating fellow enthusiasts who would, in turn, take steps to protect the land they had helped to preserve. To expand the ranks of informed defenders further, he has also made a $1 million grant to a university-based environment program. The program includes training for land trust field staff, so that they will be up to speed on new techniques for financing conservation.

Laying out a theory of change requires you to make explicit your assumptions about how the world works. Depending on the circumstances, "how the world works" can mean everything from how policy decisions are made, to whether or not organizations collaborate, to how they will actually behave. This sort of analysis can be extremely helpful in surfacing places where critical information is missing, or where your logic is shaky. Or where there is an unbridgeable gap between what would be required to achieve success (at least as you're provisionally defining it) and the resources you'd be able to put against it. In sum, it forces you to confront the question, "What would I have to believe is true in order for my theory of change to have a real shot at working?"

For example, many philanthropists assume that if they fund a pilot program that proves to be successful, other funders and organizations working on the same issue will quickly embrace and replicate it. (Basically, it's a version of the old "build a better mousetrap, and the world will beat a path to your door" theory.) In reality, however, few pilot programs actually do scale up. And even a little research into those that have done so successfully (such as YouthBuild and Success for

All) would soon reveal just how much time, effort, and money it typically took to bring that growth to fruition.

Laying out a theory of change can also help you become aware of the other players who will probably have to play a part in bringing about success. For the most part, philanthropists can accomplish little, if anything, on their own. At a minimum, success will depend on the participation of the people most directly affected by the issue you're intent on addressing; that is, the people you're trying to serve or whose ideas and opinions you're trying to influence. Often, though, the cast of essential characters will go well beyond that to include some combination of direct-service nonprofit or nongovernmental organizations, other donors and/or foundations, intermediary organizations of one kind or another, businesses, and/or government bodies. Not surprisingly, the more you understand the real-world dynamics of this landscape, the better your chances will be of developing a plausible theory of change.

SCOPING THE TERRAIN

The challenge of developing a good theory of change, and a sound philanthropic strategy, is not unlike the challenge confronting a business leader preparing to enter an entirely new market, or a mountain climber who's about to tackle a new peak. There's a landscape out there that you don't know nearly as much about as you must if you're to negotiate it successfully. So the more information you can gather to understand its idiosyncrasies, the better prepared you'll be to spot opportunities and to adapt in the face of setbacks.

The experience of a financier we know shows how expensive it can be not to scope the landscape. The financier, we'll call him Bret, decided that he wanted to devote the next phase of his professional life to "transforming the social capital markets." He had served on the boards of his university and a prominent art museum, and had been a faithful donor to a handful of local charities. He felt he knew something about the nonprofit sector, and what he knew smacked of inefficiency and waste. Contributions seemed to be spread across too many organizations, with the best ones being chronically underfunded. Wealthy donors were bombarded with solicitations, with no simple way to distinguish the good from the great. Aside from investing hours of personal time kicking the tires, he and donors like him had no efficient way of deciding how to allocate their resources. What was needed, he believed, was data.

His vision was simple and powerful: a Morningstar-like organization for the nonprofit sector. (Morningstar is a leader in providing research, including all sorts of stock and fund analyses, to for-profit investors.) He christened his creation "Donor Market" and hired two talented MBAs to help him draft a compelling business plan. The core of the concept was a "holistic rating system" based on "social impact creation," coupled with an "incentivized marketplace where donors give to the best nonprofits, and where information is freely shared." To get his new enterprise up and running, Bret committed one million dollars.

What Bret and his analysts did not do was scope the landscape. Their eighteen-page business plan contained exactly four sentences on "competition," one of which asserted that "the Donor Market business model will be the only social-impact-centered rating system for nonprofits." Although they identified a handful of the many organizations already participating in this space, they did not speak to any of them. They were absolutely convinced that their approach was innovative and better. And they were absolutely wrong.

In fact, a host of organizations had been working for years to serve as information aggregators, with the goal of helping to stimulate and rationalize flows of social capital. Other relevant players included online-giving marketplaces, big commercial donor-advised funds, private placement organizations, venture funds, and grant-making associations. And for nearly a century, of course, community foundations from New York, to Cleveland, to San Francisco, to Hawaii have been trusted sources of knowledge for local donors.

While none of these organizations was identical to Bret's Donor Market, they all had relevant real-world experience helping donors make decisions. Had Bret made an effort to learn from their experiences, he might have calibrated the feasibility of his initiative better. He would have learned that collecting accurate and timely data on hundreds of thousands of nonprofits is hardly practical, and that accurately measuring impact can be challenging to do for one organization, much less thousands. He might even have discovered that because all philanthropy is personal, data can be useful but is not necessarily determinative. Personal experience with the nonprofit and the cause is often more important.

It took Bret three years and a bit more than $600,000 in expenses before he finally called it quits. It was a high price to pay for ignorance coupled with arrogance.

Approaching philanthropy with humility and an inquiring mind will help avoid avoidable problems, as well as put your resources to the best use. And while the information relevant to your area of interest will necessarily be situation specific, there are some general questions we recommend asking:

- How do the people who are most deeply involved with this issue—the people you're aiming to serve—understand it?
- Who else is actively engaged in addressing the issue?
- What is already happening out in the world that appears to be working? What doesn't seem to be working, and why?
- What do experts have to say about why the issue persists?
- What have others tried in the past, and what lessons have they learned?
- Does the issue seem ripe for tackling now?
- Are there specific kinds of help that would be particularly useful? For example, are there organizations that merit expansion (scaling up), because they've shown they can tackle this issue successfully? Conversely, are there a lot of open questions that might be addressed by innovation and small-scale experiments (seeding the field)?

As you learn more and fill in your map, you may discover that there is a rich store of "failures" from which you can profit by learning what *not* to do. Alternatively, you may find successes from which you can also learn, or maybe even piggyback on. The objective, after all, is to solve the problem, not reinvent the wheel. As an example, consider what Jeff

Walker and his partners were able to accomplish by working with NPower.

Jeffrey Walker: Building on Success

In the spring of 1998, Jeff Walker, a New York venture capitalist, got into a conversation with several of his partners, who had gone in with him to back a number of local nonprofits. Collectively, they worried over the fact that several of the nonprofits they'd been involved with had wasted a lot of money and time building unique technology solutions. As one nonprofit executive director had recently admitted to Walker, "I lost a million dollars in technology. I don't know where it went. We got nothing for it."[25]

As Walker and his partners discussed the issue, they realized that what was needed was an organization that could share technology solutions among nonprofits. If one nonprofit figured out an effective way to develop a central donor database, they wondered, why couldn't it share that model with others?

With this germ of an idea, Walker and his partners decided to look around and see if other people and organizations were wrestling with the same problem. "Instead of starting something up to compete," Walker recalls them asking each other, "why don't we look around the country, see who else is doing something similar, and learn from them?" While conducting this informal survey, they came across NPower, a group in Seattle funded in part by Microsoft. It turned out that NPower not only did exactly the sort of thing that Walker and his colleagues wanted to back, but also was interested in rolling out a national model.

Walker helped put together the necessary funding, and the result was an NPower affiliate in New York. Since then, NPower has successfully expanded across the nation. In ten years it has helped over 25,000 nonprofits with their IT needs, including many organizations in New York.[26] Had Walker and his partners not taken the time to look around and learn more, they would never have found NPower in Seattle. They might have wasted precious resources—and not tapped into important knowledge—as they built a similar model of their own.

Scoping the landscape may also help you uncover genuine "white space," potentially plausible options or strategies that no one seems to have considered before. In fact, this was how the Michael J. Fox Foundation, established by the actor in 2000, nine years after he was diagnosed with early onset Parkinson's disease,[27] went about creating its strategy.

The Michael J. Fox Foundation: Finding Real White Space

From the outset, the Michael J. Fox Foundation has been dedicated to finding a cure for Parkinson's disease through an aggressively funded research agenda. But Fox and his colleagues, including the chief executive officer, Katie Hood, are determined not to duplicate the work of others.[28] Early in the foundation's existence, a formal "landscaping" exercise was initiated to understand where other funders' dollars were invested and to assess where the foundation's dollars could have the most impact.

This exercise persuaded the foundation to deemphasize basic research, the traditional domain of the National Institutes of Health, and instead to concentrate its efforts on filling critical gaps in the drug-development pipeline—white space where it could make an important difference. That, in turn, led the foundation to zero in on creating incentives for researchers to focus on translating discoveries into therapies, rather than on making discoveries, and to collaborate, share information, and partner in new ways in order to speed the introduction of new therapies to the market.

Because people view the foundation as an honest broker, it is in a unique position to develop a cross-field perspective, as well as to engage a diverse set of players—from celebrities to research scientists to venture capitalists—in dialogue and debate. Respect for the foundation's unique business model is such that other disease-focused foundations increasingly look to emulate its efforts.

How much of this kind of terrain scoping should you do? It all depends. The facts underpinning a theory of change can be developed in a day or a year, depending on the level of complexity of the challenge and how important it is to "get it as right as possible." In most cases, the effort you invest in scoping should be proportional to the outcome you anticipate, and the resources you intend to deploy. It is one thing to consider making a significant contribution to a capital campaign that seeks to endow an art museum or a hospital on whose board you have been active for years. It is quite another if you are hoping to help change national environmental policies or end the trade in blood diamonds but have no prior experience with those issues.

As a general rule, the larger the scale of the effort (and dollars) you're considering, the more complex the issue is. And the greater the uncertainty as to what the most important factors in propelling change will be, the more new information and hard facts you'll want to gather before you move ahead.

That said, we should also caution against "analysis paralysis." Huge amounts of data—even irrelevant data—can be comforting, even as it distracts you from the task at hand. The search for the perfect, game-changing data is almost always a trap, because those kinds of definitive directional signs rarely exist when you're asking really difficult questions.

How will you know when you're finished scoping? This is always a judgment call, and your good judgment will be what's needed. But you can be pretty sure you're close when you've gotten your strategy to the point where it can pass two practical, commonsense tests. First, the facts on the ground don't contradict the key assumptions underpinning your theory of change. Second, an objective, reasonable and knowledgeable outsider could look at your data and logic and say, "Yes, that makes sense. Based on everything I know, this strategy is doable."

DON'T UNDERESTIMATE
THE CHALLENGE

Maybe you are thinking that this all sounds straightforward and sensible, perhaps even obvious. And yet, we often see philanthropists leaping into action without having gotten clear about what will constitute success, and without having gotten real about what it will take to achieve that success.

What's the problem? Basically, the problem is human nature. It feels good to be generous, and it's flattering to be thanked for our generosity. It doesn't feel as good to impose discipline on ourselves (at least not while the discipline is being exercised) and do the kind of hard work described in this chapter. Who wants to make tough choices, especially when there are no compelling external reasons to do so? In an arena where excellence is self-imposed, we are all too inclined to set the bar low, to fall back on enticing but fuzzy definitions of success. We don't make tough trade-offs. We don't give up on pipe dreams. We don't say no to funding requests that may have only a remote chance of doing some good in addressing the issues we care most about. We are generous, but undisciplined.

If we don't say no to detours and distractions, however, our philanthropy will never amount to more than the sum of its parts. Pure luck carries philanthropy only so far. Absent a clear, thoughtful strategy, philanthropy will always underperform against its potential. Sadly, it's not unusual to come across donors who haven't been clear-headed about their desired outcomes; several years down the line, they are struggling with the nagging sense that "nothing's adding up," or worse, with the growing conviction that "nothing has changed."

A now infamous example of philanthropic underperformance is the Annenberg Challenge. In December 1993, former ambassador to Great Britain Walter Annenberg issued a $500 million challenge to communities across the United States to improve their public schools.[29] The challenge required Annenberg funds to be matched by contributions from other foundations. It also precluded grants directly to school districts, which meant that funding could go only to outside groups with school-reform projects in mind. However, Annenberg provided no clarity around the results he hoped to see achieved, nor did he specify the approaches he hoped to see tested. As a result, the grant administrators were free to deploy the funds entirely as they saw fit.

Ultimately, eighteen locally designated projects were funded in thirty-five states and 2,400 public schools, serving more than 1.5 million students and 80,000 teachers.[30] Impressive numbers, but less than impressive results: five years after launch, the Annenberg Foundation deemed only two of the initiatives worthy of renewal (and another partner funder later described one of the two as "a Rube Goldberg effort").[31]

That said, it is hard to label the Annenberg Challenge a failure. For one thing, it generated more than $600 million in matching grants from local sources, achieving a previously unprecedented level of public and private partnership around education. As important, because of Annenberg's commitment to evaluation and public sharing of results, two decades of philanthropists and educators have been able to learn from his experience. Instead of burying the disappointing results as many philanthropists do, Annenberg had the courage to be upfront about the outcomes and (insofar as it was known) why things had gone wrong.[32]

In addition to achieving clarity around what constitutes success, donors also need to guard against underestimating the difficulty of things they don't know a lot about, and overestimating how much they (and their colleagues) do know. Passionate philanthropists are impatient people; as one donor memorably put it, "Children are dying while we're dithering!" But letting passion and impatience lead you into doing too little homework, or reaching superficial strategic conclusions, or mistaking opinions for facts is also a recipe for underperformance.

When ignorance permeates your decision making, you are setting off on a long hike in unknown terrain without a compass—and you are almost certain to get lost. This is especially troublesome in philanthropy, because it is a sphere in which you can get lost and not even know it. All too often, philanthropists who are demonstrably lost give themselves an "A" for their efforts, declare victory, and move on to new challenges. The only people who spot the underlying failures are those who needed help, and didn't get it.

Ignorance is the paramount philanthropic sin. Arrogance is its twin. Whether you are a donor, trustee, or senior foundation officer, arrogance poses a clear and present danger. As the old saying goes, "He or she who has the gold has the power." And where there is power, arrogance trails not far behind.

The last lesson of this chapter, therefore, is to resist underestimating the strategic challenge of moving from aspirations to impact. Discipline yourself to do good well. Push back on these natural but undesirable human tendencies. Invest the necessary effort to get clear about your definition of success. And be as smart as possible about how that success might be achieved with and through others, so that you can increase the odds of leveraging your scarce resources to make a significant difference in the world.

3

WHAT AM I
ACCOUNTABLE FOR?

THE NUMBER OF PHILANTHROPISTS WHO DE-
mand accountability of their grantees is growing by
leaps and bounds. Yet the number of philanthropists
who demand accountability of themselves remains extremely
small. This is a lost opportunity. Why? Because confronting
the question "What am I accountable for?" is not only the
best way to pressure test your philanthropic strategy, but also
the key to delivering the results you intend to achieve. And
it applies equally to individual donors and foundation executives.

When we take accountability seriously—whether it's to
our families and friends, colleagues at work, or teammates—
we tend to make very sure that we're clear about what's
expected of us, and that we're ready to play our part. Accountability in philanthropy is no different. When we are truly prepared to hold ourselves accountable for success, we're likely
to do everything we can to ensure that the resources we contribute are commensurate to the results we're committed to
achieve.

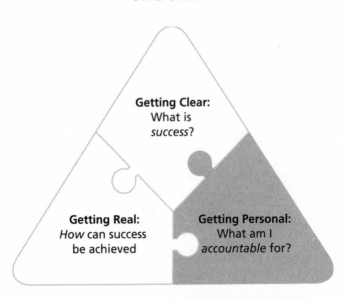

Getting Clear:
What is
success?

Getting Real:
How can success
be achieved

Getting Personal:
What am I
accountable for?

In the previous chapter, we looked at the challenge of striking this balance as objectively as possible, in the context of getting clear ("what is success?") and getting real ("how can it be achieved?"). Now the imperative is to get personal. By this we mean revisiting your strategy one more time, with yourself and your resources squarely in the foreground, then testing its plausibility by asking whether you'd be able and willing—no kidding—to hold yourself accountable for its success.

Why do we think getting personal is so important that it warrants its own chapter? Because in philanthropy excellence is self-imposed. Unless you demand outstanding performance from yourself, no one else will demand it of you. This terrible truth not only leaves you highly susceptible to underperformance (and disappointment) when the results of your philanthropy are all in, but also increases the risk of shortchanging the very people or issues you are hoping to serve.

Deciding what you will do to make change happen is a choice that requires both your head and your heart. The appropriate strategy for any given philanthropic initiative will be the one in line with your scarce resources: your money, your time, and your influence. It will build on your strengths. And it will be personally satisfying, because it will require contributions that you are willing, as well as able, to make.

WHAT RESOURCES AM I ABLE TO DEPLOY?

Say the word "philanthropy" and money is the first, and often the only, resource that comes to people's minds. One could make the case that, stripped of rhetoric, the essence of philanthropy is allocating scarce financial resources to the initiatives that will yield the highest good for society. But whether you agree with that statement or not, it is at best incomplete. At the end of the day, money is basically a commodity, and private wealth, however staggering the amount, pales beside the complex problems that many philanthropists and foundations are working to address. So if you are really determined to maximize the impact of your giving, you will want to define the resources you can bring to your efforts as broadly as possible. This means starting with money, but not stopping there.

Just as equity investments can be leveraged by debt in the financial world, philanthropic dollars can be leveraged by nonfinancial contributions in the world of philanthropy. Chief among these contributions are the gift of time and the use of influence, which includes the skills and expertise you've developed over a lifetime, as well as your reputation and personal and professional networks. Whether, where, and how these intangible assets can be helpful will vary. It will depend on the situation and needs of the organizations and individuals with whom you decide to work, not to mention your particular theory of change. But as you think about what you could contribute to achieving results, it's important to factor in the intangible assets on your balance sheet as well as the financial ones—and to do so in the context of the commitments you have already made across your philanthropic portfolio.

As we've noted before, we've chosen in this book to talk about decision making largely through the lens of a single philanthropic initiative or strategy. In reality, though, most philanthropists pursue a portfolio of interests, which means that the choices they make in one area necessarily affect what they can do elsewhere. In other words, they involve fundamental trade-offs.

How many areas of interest you can support, and how many will be *too* many, are questions that can only be answered on a case by case basis, given your resources and the trade-offs you're willing to make about using them. In the business world, when strategists write about making trade-offs, they normally preach the power of "focus," and urge executives to concentrate their resources around a few attractive markets that build upon a strong competitive position. But in philanthropy, a more concentrated portfolio doesn't invariably lead to higher impact. In other words, for any given level of resources, two initiatives are not automatically better than four.

The critical imperative is to remember that there is no such thing as an isolated philanthropic decision. Every new commitment will require trade-offs, not only around the amount of money it will involve, but also around the demands it may place on your time or willingness to use your influence. Making those decisions explicit is far better than allowing them to go unexamined. Otherwise, you run the risk of inadvertently finding yourself overcommitted on the one hand, or engaged in "peanut butter philanthropy"—with your money, time, and influence spread at a more or less uniform thinness across too many activities—on the other.

Finally, you may also want to consider leaving at least a little of your capacity uncommitted, so that you can take advantage of new opportunities as they arise. This is a wise course, because it allows you to respond rapidly to important but unanticipated funding opportunities. It also gives you flexibility to respond to what you're learning from your current grant making and to double down when circumstances warrant increased investment. The difference between the approaches to education reform pursued by foundation funders in the 1980s and 1990s offers a good example.

The foundations that participated in the earlier wave of education reform tended to select and fund specific ideas all at once. This reduced the possibility of supporting alternative, and potentially more successful, concepts that emerged later on. By contrast, the foundations that led the charge in the 1990s "kept their powder dry." They initially supported a limited number of experiments (such as charter schools and school vouchers) on a small scale. As a result, they were well positioned to make larger commitments when good ideas began to prove themselves.[1]

With these overarching comments as a backdrop, let's look more closely at the three scarce resources every philanthropist possesses to one degree or another: money, time, and influence.

MAKING THE MOST OF YOUR MONEY

Philanthropy's core activity historically has been giving money away, and that continues to account for the lion's share of philanthropic dollars. For every $100 of assets, moreover, most established foundations expend about $5 per year—a level that satisfies the mandatory 5 percent "payout" required by law. That amount includes the money going to grantees (for illustrative purposes, say $4), as well as justifiable administrative expenses (the remaining $1 in our simple example). This book is focused largely on how to help make your philanthropy—the $4 going to your grantees—generate better results. In subsequent chapters, we will address a number of important questions around that $4, including, in chapter four, the need to invest appropriately in capacity building.

However, a small but growing number of donors are complementing (or even replacing) traditional giving with other ways of using financial resources to catalyze social change. Our purpose in discussing this dynamic topic is to prompt you to consider the question "How can I best put my money to work to achieve success?" broadly and creatively, rather than necessarily limit yourself solely to more common practices.

For starters, what about the $1 spent on grant-related expenses? Much of that may be the direct administrative burden required to support your philanthropy (a figure that would be far smaller if, for instance, you worked through a community foundation or your own donor-advised fund). But suppose you were to use some portion of that $1 expense to help achieve success—to generate results much like the $4 given directly to the grantee. You might decide to employ experienced program managers to work with grantees, for instance, or to hire consultants to provide technical assistance or leadership training. Or you might invest in a wide range of valuable activities, from technology development, to research, to measurement and evaluation, to hosting conferences. Although these expenses may reduce the amount of money available for grants (that is, encroach on the $4), there is nothing sacrosanct about the balance between money you give away to get results and expenses you might incur to achieve those same ends. A donor engaged in advocacy, for example, might find it much more effective to spend money directly on a communications campaign than give incrementally more money to a nonprofit advocacy organization. This simple but subtle point—spending money in addition to giving it away—can be an effective approach to generating better results.

Another way that donors try to make the most of their money is by aggregating capital, combining their $4 of giving with other people's money. Many sorts of nonprofit organizations (including local churches and the Salvation Army) have essentially been "aggregating" charitable capital for years through their fund-raising efforts. One of the oldest true practitioners is the United Way of America, founded in 1887, which aggregates capital through its workplace campaigns.[2] In this case, contributions from individual donors are pooled to help address the pressing needs of local communities. The large-scale capital campaigns now common among colleges and universities provide vibrant illustrations of organizations aggressively pooling individual contributions around shared institutional goals.

In recent years, however, another powerful form of capital aggregation has gained prominence: strategic alliances among institutional donors designed to provide growth capital and/or tackle significant social problems. The Edna McConnell Clark Foundation's Growth Capital Aggregation Pilot offers an example of the first; ClimateWorks illustrates the second.

For more than a decade, the Edna McConnell Clark Foundation has focused its grant making on youth-serving nonprofits whose programs have been proven effective, with the goal of helping them reach greater numbers of young people in need. Recognizing that their grantees' ability to scale up was severely hampered by the lack of significant amounts of up-front capital, the foundation launched its pioneering Growth Capital Aggregation Pilot in 2008.

Using stringent selection criteria, the foundation's leadership chose three grantees, Nurse-Family Partnership, Youth Villages, and Citizen Schools, to participate in the pilot. Aiming to create a $120 million pool of funds, Clark committed $39 million of funding and actively supported the grantees to secure the other $81 million. In less than six months, the funds had been raised, with nineteen coinvestors (including both institutions and individual donors) signing a Memorandum of Understanding. The document establishes joint terms, performance metrics, shared reporting, and a financial model that allows grantees to draw down funds only if they achieve agreed-upon milestones. Clark expects that by 2012 this $120 million in private funds will help the organizations leverage an additional $700 million in public funds.[3]

In 2007, six foundations with a shared concern about global warming commissioned a study that sought to answer a critical question: "What would it take to achieve a real 'win' in the battle against climate change?" The study, Design to

Win: Philanthropy's Role in the Fight Against Global Warming, led to a $1 billion commitment on the part of the William and Flora Hewlett Foundation, the McKnight Foundation, and the David and Lucille Packard Foundation to fund ClimateWorks Foundation, a new nonprofit with the goal of cutting greenhouse gas emissions in half by 2030. Together with a global family of affiliated organizations, ClimateWorks Foundation is working to support public policies that will prevent climate change and promote sustainable economic development.[4]

Innovative philanthropists are also exploring how to use more of the assets on their balance sheets to finance social change (that is, some of the remaining $95 in our simplified illustration that they don't customarily expend every year). In 2009, the Bill & Melinda Gates Foundation announced plans to offer $400 million in loans, equity investments, and loan guarantees in addition to its traditional grant making. The action signals a shift by the world's largest philanthropic organization to tie part of its $30 billion in assets directly to grantees, rather than simply handing out a share of the investment income from its endowment.

"We are using a conservative approach to leverage our balance sheet," said Alexander Friedman, the foundation's chief financial officer and a former investment banker. "This gives us a $400 million envelope beyond our program budget of firepower to do deals for the poor."[5]

In 2010, some of these funds were used for underwriting bonds with Aspire Public Schools, a top charter school network in California. The Gates Foundation and the Charles and Helen Schwab Corporation each provided $8 million in guarantees to back $93 million in bonds for Aspire, which will help provide permanent facilities for the schools' use. Besides helping Aspire serve four thousand students annually, the funds allowed it to secure a better loan rate, which could end up saving the organization more than $11 million over the life of the loans.[6]

Other donors are both leveraging their balance sheets and pooling capital. For example, five separate foundations recently pooled their resources to provide the first tier of risk capital for a development initiative by the New York City Housing Authority (NYCHA). The NYCHA aims to provide decent and affordable housing in safe environments for low- and moderate-income residents in New York City.[7] Housing in New York City is a notoriously expensive endeavor, requiring significant investment capital for maintenance and modernization.[8] "Guarantee pools," such as the one the foundations created, secure the loans made to a developer against default, thereby diminishing risk for later investors.[9] In this case, these initial investments helped attract many additional funders, including some New York City banks that contributed $250 million for a second tier of loan guarantees. With these funds, the NYCHA built 30,000 units of affordable housing.

"Mission-related investing" is a term that encompasses a range of activities and vehicles aimed at using assets to further a specific social mission. Various approaches include program-related investments, loan guarantees, and other forms of collateralization, as well as portfolio investments designed to generate both social and financial returns. In this latter category, for example, an environmental philanthropist may decide not only to avoid investing in companies that cause environmental damage, but also to go a step further and invest in businesses that are actually developing clean energy sources, like wind or solar. Similarly, a donor intent on addressing urban poverty may simultaneously give money to nonprofit organizations assisting the poor, while also using investment funds to provide venture capital to small business start-ups in distressed urban areas.

Omidyar Network (ON) illustrates where this kind of thinking can lead. ON, which refers to itself as a "philanthropic investment firm," invests in for-profit socially oriented businesses, while also making grants to nonprofit organizations.[10] "We start from the premise that we want to invest flexible capital," says managing partner Matt Bannick. "We start by developing a real understanding of the problem, and then decide what would be the most appropriate type of capital to deploy."[11]

An example of this dual approach is ON's support of BRAC, a Bangladeshi-based development organization focused on poverty alleviation, which is one of the largest NGOs in the world. ON and its sister organization Humanity United have given BRAC both philanthropic and investment capital for its work in Sierra Leone and Liberia; they have made equity investments to support the launch of microfinance operations in both countries; and they are providing grants for local health volunteers who dispense basic care and treatments for diseases such as malaria, tuberculosis, and cholera.

Interestingly, Jeff Skoll, the first president of eBay, has also taken an investment-related approach to driving social change. His business, Participant Media, has produced hit documentaries like *An Inconvenient Truth*, which highlighted the threat of global warming, and *Waiting for Superman*, which emphasized the importance of transforming U.S. education.

As Skoll explains, "When we look at a project, first we see if it's a good story well told. Can it be commercially viable? Will people go see it? But, more importantly, will the social change that results from the film be greater than the capital we're putting in? For us, the theatrical release is just the start of the social action"[12]

While documentaries like *Waiting for Superman* show clear links to social issues, all of Participant's films are accompanied by social action agendas. *North Country,* for instance, is a 2005 feature film about one of the early major sexual harassment cases in the United States. Participant timed its release to coincide with the vote on the reauthorization of the Violence Against Women Act. For another film, *Charlie Wilson's War,* Participant worked with veterans' groups to help promote programs providing education, health, and mental health services for veterans.[13] Participant has even identified six focus areas (as a foundation might) with which chosen films must align.[14]

The conceptual line between philanthropy and investing can become pretty blurred, pretty fast. Richard Branson, the founder of the British conglomerate Virgin Group, made global headlines in 2006 when he declared he would dedicate $3 billion to helping solve the climate crisis. Announced at the Clinton Global Initiative annual event, his commitment was clearly focused on a critical social issue.[15] Yet Branson was clear that this was not a charitable endeavor, but a for-profit initiative focused on investing in clean technologies such as wind turbines and cleaner-burning aviation fuel.

Reflecting a similar investment thesis, venture capital firm Kleiner Perkins launched its $500 million Green Growth Fund in 2008 to "help speed the mass market adoption of solutions to the climate crisis." While the fund has a clear social purpose, it is not altruistic: Kleiner had clearly calculated that this investment strategy would produce significant returns for its investors relative to other possibilities.[16]

Fully considering the question of allocating assets between philanthropy and investments that earn satisfactory returns as well as help to address social problems is beyond the scope of this book. Philanthropy cannot substitute for the power of markets. Throughout the modern era, marketplaces have driven higher standards of living, and the innovations that have led to better lives. This fundamental truth is evident today in China, as that country's economic prosperity lifts hundreds of millions of citizens out of poverty. But philanthropy can creatively address market failure: places where market forces produce undesirable consequences, or where market forces alone cannot solve social problems. So as you consider how to make the most of your money, it's useful to think hard about which problems naturally lend themselves to philanthropic solutions, and which might be better addressed by other means.

MAKING THE MOST OF YOUR TIME

People have widely varying amounts of wealth, but we all have the same twenty-four hours in a day. How you will deploy this scarce resource is one of your most important strategic decisions, whether you are a part-time philanthropist or a full-time foundation leader.

When Peter Lynch and his wife, Carolyn, were raising their children, and he was establishing his reputation as a legendary money manager at Fidelity Investments, much of their philanthropy revolved around responding to existing organizations doing good work on issues they cared deeply about. When Lynch turned forty-six, however, mindful of the fact that his father had died unexpectedly at the same age, he made a conscious decision to reorder his priorities.[17] By 1988, as the professional and personal demands on the Lynches began to ease, they were in a position to establish a foundation to which they could commit significant amounts of time. Since then, they have been increasingly hands-on in their philanthropy—reviewing proposals, assessing impact, and making introductions between grantees and other potential funders.[18]

In contrast, many philanthropists are still in the position the Lynches were in when they started out, with work and family responsibilities consuming the lion's share of their days. Muneer Satter, a managing director at Goldman Sachs is one such person. Although his career is extremely demanding, Satter is committed to finding ways to be directly engaged in his philanthropy. "I have no staff in my foundation," he says, "because I still want to be involved personally—write the checks myself, do the due diligence myself, do the learning myself."[19]

Choosing grantees with outstanding leaders is one of the ways Satter has found to leverage his time. "I have to try to pick good people. If I see an interesting idea, I can't hire and oversee hundreds of people to manage it, and I can't run long studies to test it. I focus on finding good people who are good leaders that I can trust to fulfill their missions." Because his own involvement and participation are necessarily limited, Satter uses his time to make sure that the leaders of the nonprofits he chooses to fund have both the capabilities and the capacity to support their organizations in the ways needed for success.

Josh Bekenstein, a managing director and early leader of Bain Capital, illustrates another way to pursue results when you cannot devote much time to your philanthropy. Through a long-term relationship (including cochairing its board) with New Profit, a national venture philanthropy group, he has been able to stay sharply focused on results. New Profit aggregates philanthropic capital. It also vets and selects social entrepreneurs and organizations with high potential to address issues like education, public health, and poverty alleviation, which have a huge impact on social mobility.[20] Organizations that make it through New Profit's rigorous due diligence process receive significant support, thanks to the funds in New Profit's philanthropic investment portfolio.

Bekenstein points out that intermediaries like New Profit can be valuable for many of today's philanthropists: "If you're a philanthropic individual, and you don't have a staff, how do you decide which of the fifty social entrepreneurs knocking on your door should get your money? You could just divide it fifty ways, but that would be a poor way to do it. Through New Profit, more individuals can get involved in social entrepreneurial organizations making a difference."[21]

Every commitment of time is personal and unique. But some realities seem to apply across the board. One of the most iron clad is that if you are a committed philanthropist who has decided to spend more of your time in a specific arena (taking on a leadership role in the context of a larger-scale initiative, for instance) it's a safe bet that the demands on your time will only increase, and that success will likely increase those demands even further. At the same time, there are still only twenty-four hours in a day. Thinking these constraints through *before* taking on new commitments will go a long way toward helping you meet your new obligations.

Conscious of these constraints, philanthropists Sandy and Joan Weill choose to devote a great deal of time to only a few organizations. "For us," Sandy notes, "it's not running in and out with these groups. It's not just about giving money or spreading it thin. Philanthropy is really about a lot of hard work, passion and believing in something, and spending lots of time on it."[22]

The Weills' commitments bring those words to life. In 1982, Sandy founded the National Academy Foundation, which supports a national network of career academies to help develop America's youth; he has led its board ever since. Joan is currently chairman of the board of the Alvin Ailey American Dance Foundation Inc., a position she has held for a decade. Sandy has served as the chair of the Carnegie Hall board for twenty years as well as the chair of Weill Cornell Medical College for almost fifteen years.

Time is an equally important and sensitive resource for senior foundation staff, who are continually confronted with an array of competing responsibilities. When your philanthropy is foundation based, your institution's norms and requirements (unwritten as well as written) inevitably bound what *can* be done, and establish expectations around what *must* be done. For example, is it your job to get money out the door in order to "make your numbers"? Or is it, say, to add value to key initiatives by serving as an advisor on the organization's management? These choices will be strongly influenced not only by the average size and duration of a foundation's grants, but also by factors like the board's priorities and the level of internal support staff members receive.

Similarly, how much of your time is devoted to making new grants versus managing prior commitments (and adding value to current grantees)? What is the mix (real and hoped for) between internal responsibilities and external field-building? Between strategy development and daily foundation processes? How much of your time should be invested in external collaborations with other donors and key partners?

The consequences of not being thoughtful about real trade-offs like these can be staggering. We once did a back-of-the-envelope calculation of the full requirements being placed on a group of foundation program directors. By specifying those requirements in detail, we found that they amounted to over ninety hours per week.

In our experience, individual philanthropists and foundation staffers alike tend to exaggerate the amount of time they can actually contribute to any given initiative. Their intentions are good, but in many cases all the hours they hoped to spend somehow fail to materialize. They are pushed backward, into prior commitments that have either taken off or gotten into trouble, or pulled forward into the next new thing. Your goal, therefore, should be to be brutally honest with yourself (and others) about the commitments you have already made and then, within those constraints, to decide what (if anything) more you are capable of contributing.

MAKING THE MOST OF YOUR INFLUENCE

Your skills and knowledge, your reputation, your expertise, your personal and professional networks: using these intangible assets to spur people to do things they otherwise would not, or could not, do goes to the heart of what we mean by influence. In 1986, Ray Chambers stepped down from Wesray Capital Corporation, the pioneering leveraged-buyout firm he cofounded with former U.S. Treasury secretary William Simon. His career since then offers a compelling example of the ways in which influence can be used to drive change.

Chambers's philanthropic activities began in Newark, New Jersey, where he was born and raised. The city's social fabric had disintegrated in the aftermath of bloody riots in 1967, as had its schools, cultural facilities, and economic and political infrastructure. His first undertaking involved working with the new director of the city's Boys & Girls Clubs, Barbara Wright Bell, to renovate four facilities that had been overrun by gangs. He helped the organization find new sources of funds that quadrupled its budget and also attracted influential board members. "I had never seen people as down and out as the people of Newark," he observed. "It had gotten so bad, I didn't think I had any alternative."[23]

Chambers quickly became engaged in a variety of rebuilding efforts, including the establishment of the state's first performing arts center and the creation of mentoring and scholarship programs for some of Newark's neediest children. In 1990, when then President Bush asked him to become the founding chairman of the Points of Light Foundation, his philanthropy grew to encompass national projects: the National Mentoring Partnership (now known as MENTOR), which he cofounded with Geoff Boisi, and America's Promise Alliance, cofounded with General Colin Powell.

Most recently, he has been instrumental in shaping the Millennium Promise Alliance, created to raise awareness and financial support to fight global poverty, hunger, and disease, and Malaria No More, which seeks to neutralize the threat of malaria. As the canvas for his philanthropy has expanded, he continues to draw on the skills and knowledge that made him successful in business: the expert use of financial leverage to grow the funds available to do good; his mastery of coalition building; his willingness to call on his extensive personal network—and the mutual respect that encourages people to return his calls. And, perhaps most important of all, his ability to excite and motivate others to band together in creating something new.

Getting people to contribute money and/or time to the organizations you care about, as Chambers does, is a powerful way to use your influence. But the more you think expansively—and listen attentively to the needs of those you're working with—the longer the menu of possibilities is likely to grow. It might include something as directly personal (and one-to-one) as drawing on the skills you've developed in your professional life to provide coaching for a high-performing, but inexperienced, nonprofit leader. Or the focus might be on using your expertise to advance the impact of the organizations you support, as Jean Case has done through the Case Foundation, which she cofounded with her husband, Steve, in 1997.

Jean, Steve, and their business colleagues helped transform online space from an exotic neighborhood to an almost ubiquitous digital resource, through the successful development and expansion of America Online, Inc. When she first entered the philanthropic world in 1997, Jean assumed that she would have to "change her stripes"—that is, stop being a businessperson and start being a philanthropist. Quickly, though, she realized that being someone who was "intensely focused and passionate around technology" might be a *good* thing in the philanthropic realm.[24]

One grantee that has benefited from the Cases' technology expertise is Network for Good, a Web platform that enables online donations to thousands of charities. Network for Good's start up in 2001 was supported by a rare industry collaboration among companies including AOL, Cisco, and Yahoo! In the years since, the Case Foundation has provided Network for Good with grants and lent expertise through strategic planning support and service on its board. Since its inception, Network for Good has raised over $400 million for more than 50,000 charities.[25]

The Case's technology expertise has also inspired innovative approaches to basic foundation processes, like grant making. Its Make It Your Own awards relied on recommendations and votes from more than 15,000 individuals and community nonprofits to suggest and screen grant recipients for a specific pool of funds.[26] This "crowdsourcing" approach to choosing grantees has not only replaced the traditional grant application process, but also enabled a new kind of citizen-centered philanthropy.

An historic, and still instructive, example of applying professional skills to philanthropic endeavors comes from Albert and Mary Lasker, who established the Lasker Foundation in 1942 with the stated goal of supporting medical research.[27] The Laskers not only donated their own funds, but also drew on a lesson learned during Albert's service in the federal government during the early 1920s—to apply pressure to Congress to direct large amounts of federal dollars toward medical research.

The Laskers were particularly focused on fighting cancer, which had affected them both in a number of ways. One of the challenges they faced was that in the mid-1940s, "cancer" was still a taboo subject in polite society. Drawing on his experience and connections in the advertising and broadcast realms, Albert arranged to have the lead characters in a then wildly popular radio show, *Fibber McGee and Molly*, talk openly about cancer. "Cancer isn't a thing that will go away if you close your eyes," Fibber told his friend Charley. "Cancer isn't a disgrace; it's a disgrace to think it's a disgrace."[28]

The example of Mary and Albert Lasker illustrates the way that your reputation and influence, including the professional networks you've developed through your work in business, government, or institutional philanthropy, can be used as a philanthropic resource. Judith Rodin, president of the Rockefeller Foundation, and Darren Walker, the former vice president of Foundation Initiatives, provide a contemporary example.[29]

Within days of Hurricane Katrina's devastation of the Gulf Coast in August 2005, the Rockefeller leadership announced grants of more than $3 million that were to be disbursed to community-based organizations. Even more critical than this quick response, however, was their ability to tap into Rockefeller's convening power some months later, when it looked as though the New Orleans planning process had stalled. Drawing on the foundation's strong existing network in New Orleans, Rodin and Walker helped bring key actors together around the creation of a central recovery plan. Rockefeller was also able to bring to the table a substantial body of knowledge around urban renewal, acquired through its years of support for the Living Cities initiative, a philanthropic collaborative aimed at revitalizing America's cities. The Unified New Orleans Plan was eventually approved in June 2007, unlocking nearly $200 million in government recovery funds—a massive return on Rockefeller's own grants of under $10 million, enabled largely by its thoughtful use of reputation and influence.[30]

You needn't be the size of the Rockefeller Foundation, however, in order to use your influence to make things happen. One of the most helpful services individual donors and institutional funders can render their grantees is introducing them to others who might become future supporters. Drawing on your personal network to identify and recruit strong candidates for a grantee's board or agreeing to chair a capital campaign are other contributions that can be enormously valuable. The most important thing is being willing to think expansively about the personal assets you may not even realize you have, and how you could deploy them to help achieve success.

WHAT RESOURCES AM I WILLING TO DEPLOY?

Just because you *can* do something doesn't necessarily mean that you'll be *willing* to do it.

Your reputation and network could give you the potential to raise a lot of money, for example, but you might loathe being the person who has to make the "ask." Similarly, you could have great access to politicians whose support would be helpful in passing a key piece of legislation, but engaging in backroom politics may not be how you want to spend your time. So once you're clear about what you could do to advance the prospects of success, you need to get equally clear about what you're willing to do—not just in terms of using your influence, but also with respect to your money and time.

This means thinking less about your capacity and more about your personal preferences. Not least among these is what you consider fun: activities that make your days exciting and your weeks fulfilling. That may sound as though we're advising you to be self-indulgent. In reality, it is anything but. If the philanthropic responsibilities you take on aren't personally rewarding, you aren't likely to persist. And in philanthropy (as in many other aspects of life), getting to results not only tends to cost more than we initially expected, but usually takes more time and effort as well.

This inescapable fact of life points to two other personal considerations that need to be factored in as you think about what you're willing to do to achieve results: your time frame for involvement and your tolerance for risk.

What's my time frame? Some results can be achieved relatively quickly, while others can take a decade, if not longer. A preschool reading-readiness program can produce successful outcomes in one year, yet it might require several years of seed funding to "import" and incubate a program that has worked elsewhere into your own city. When Jean and Steve Case and other funders in the Washington, DC, area helped bring City Year to the national capitol region, for example, they recognized that the fledgling organization would need significant help during its start-up years. Together, these funders agreed to provide seed funding for three to five years to get City Year off the ground.[31]

At the other end of the spectrum, and it is a broad spectrum, is the Rockefeller Foundation's funding of the "green revolution."[32] Rockefeller's commitment to improving agricultural productivity in the developing world began with an initial outlay of $20,000 in 1943, aimed at surveying crop yields in Mexico. In the following year, the foundation contributed $192,800 to the Mexican Agricultural Project, in conjunction with the Mexican Ministry of Agriculture. By 1956, Mexico was self-sufficient in wheat. Rockefeller agreed to fund similar programs throughout Latin America, and also in India where, together with the U.S. Agency for International Development and the U.S. Department of Agriculture, it established five state agriculture universities. With the help of the Ford Foundation and other funders, a Rockefeller-led team began developing high-yield crops for the South Asian environment. This effort led to the awarding of the 1970 Nobel Peace Prize to team leader Dr. Norman Borlaug. Today, high-yield agriculture is credited with saving over a billion lives since the 1960s.[33]

The imperative here is to be as realistic as possible on two counts: how long it's likely to take to achieve the results you want to see, and how long you're prepared to stay involved. When it comes to "moving the needle" in fields like poverty, the environment, or maternal and child health, remarkably little can be accomplished in eighteen months. And yet, the majority of philanthropic grants run for two years or less. In most cases, it makes no more sense to set a standard (and necessarily arbitrary) time limit for all your grants than it would to set a standard sum of money to award. In both instances, specific circumstances should dictate the approach.

Donors intent on achieving results need to be up-front,

clear-minded, and realistic about matching the time frames for their grants with what they're trying to accomplish. Many of the problems philanthropists address require multiyear, or even multidecade, solutions. Few are able (even if they might be willing) to make commitments of such length. If there is a clear and sizable discrepancy between the time required to achieve even interim results and your own time frame for commitment, you may want to pause and double back to your definition of success before moving on to think about your appetite for risk, and for accountability.

Being thoughtful about risk. One of the most compelling arguments for maintaining the broad freedom from external accountability that philanthropists enjoy is that it affords them the freedom to experiment and take risks—risks that business and government entities cannot, or will not, accept. In fact, philanthropy has served as society's "risk capital" for more than a century, in ways that range from mapping the oceans to mapping the genome, enlivening communities to enlivening the arts.

Risk is often a necessary ingredient in achieving success, especially with large complex strategies. But while it is common to come across statements such as "we pursue high-risk, high-return philanthropy," it is less common to come across evidence that the person or institution making the claim has carefully considered the real risks associated with a particular initiative, and how they might be thoughtfully managed—much less what additional results these added risks are intended to produce.

How much risk and what kinds of risk you're willing to embrace are important personal or institutional choices. In philanthropy (as in finance), they will probably differ across your portfolio. For every grant or initiative that is truly high risk, for example, you might want to have others where the path to success is much clearer. For instance, providing funds for a program or organization, perhaps in collaboration with others, that has already demonstrated its ability to produce results. Or you may decide to balance big multiyear bets addressing complex challenges like health care with annual giving that supports local nonprofits focused on meeting neighborhood needs.

Conversely, if your inclination is to mitigate risk as much as possible (by, say, working exclusively in situations where it's easy to draw the connection between your contribution and tangible results), you may discover that "playing it safe" creates its own unintended risk: namely, the risk that your philanthropy will underperform.

As you reflect on your tolerance for risk, and where the gift or grant you are considering fits within it, there are three different but often overlapping kinds of risk to think about: strategic risk, secondary risk, and personal risk. We'll look at each briefly in turn.

Strategic risk is the risk that your efforts will come to naught; that the resources you have invested either fail to generate any results whatsoever, or that the results are, at best, unsatisfactory. At a minimum, you waste your money (as well as whatever time and influence you have expended on the initiative). At worst, your efforts do unintended (and perhaps avoidable) harm to others.

Strategic risk is largely a function of three elements: the scale of the effort being contemplated (your definition of success); the complexity of the issue being targeted (the number

What is your appetite for strategic risk?

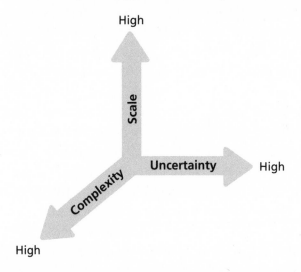

Scale: Magnitude of the success you hope to achieve and/or the level of resources you intend to commit.

Complexity: Inherent difficulty of theory of change, including the number and range of relevant constituents, amount of behavioral change, cause and effect relationships, and time frames.

Uncertainty: Level of confidence regarding the key assumptions underpinning the theory of change. What has and has not been proven. What is and is not knowable.

of factors that may contribute to its persistence, for example, or the number of players who will have to be involved in reaching a solution); and the degree of uncertainty the strategy contains (the inherent reliability of your theory of change). As a general rule, the larger the scale, the greater the degree of complexity; and the more uncertainty a strategy involves, the greater the risk that something, or more likely multiple things, will play out in unanticipated ways.

A theory of change is a *theory,* remember, and not a proven formula. There is always a fundamental risk that it will be flawed; that the world simply will not work as you imagined it would. This doesn't mean rejecting audacious goals with lots of unknowns—reducing the incidence of childhood obesity in disadvantaged neighborhoods, for example, or promoting multilateral treaties to reduce nuclear proliferation—out of hand. It does mean being thoughtful about trying to manage some of the risk inherent in the strategy for achieving those goals. By starting out with one or two pilot projects, for instance. And by continuing to engage in active learning as you go, so that as issues arise, they can be addressed promptly rather than be deferred until it's far too late to recoup.

That said, the strategy you're pursuing doesn't have to be out-sized or highly complicated to be risky. The Los Angeles–based Durfee Foundation seeks to support individual artists at pivotal moments in their life's work through its Artists' Resource for Completion (ARC) program. Recognizing the diversity and depth of the arts, and the absence of any standard path for forging a successful artistic career, the foundation mitigates the uncertainty inherent in selecting grant recipients in two ways. One is by awarding grants only to artists who have specific opportunities (such as a performance or an exhibition) lined up within the next six months. Another is by providing sums large enough to be helpful to the individual, but small enough that, if some grants are disappointments, they don't consume significant resources. As President Carrie Avery describes it, "Risk-taking has been part of this foundation since its beginning, and we are very comfortable with it. But we strive to be thoughtful about this balance."[34]

While strategic risk is usually the result of things not going according to your plan, *secondary risk*, or the risk you create for others, can exist even when your plan succeeds. As an illustration, consider the green revolution, cited above. Over the years, criticism has been leveled at the initiative from a variety of camps. Environmentalists have decried the overuse of fertilizers. Social scientists have pointed out that many of the benefits of new seed varieties and agricultural advances have accrued to wealthy farmers, rather than poor ones. Advocates of population control have worried that increasing the food supply has allowed nations to sidestep the tough issue of birth control.

Our point here is not an endorsement of the critics' view.* Rather, it is that even dramatic successes, like the green revolution, can generate risks with unintended, and negative, consequences. So it is always wise to think through as many "what if" scenarios as possible before launching any philanthropic venture, including "what might the unforeseen consequences be if we succeed?"

Asking "what if" questions can also help donors avoid creating unnecessary strategic risks for their grantees, other donors, and/or the issues they most care about. Advocating aggressively for a flawed theory of change, for example, can undermine the progress in a field or inappropriately skew government funding. We'll explore the unintended consequences of donors' decisions on their grantees more fully in the next two chapters. For now, though, let's look briefly at

---

*There are certainly ready answers to many of these criticisms; for example, that using the agricultural technologies of the 1950s to produce the harvest of 2000 would have required an additional 2.75 billion acres of land.

an example that many nonprofit leaders will find all too familiar.

Whether individual donors or institutional funders, philanthropists are notorious for getting all fired up about creating new programs and organizations, then losing interest once those initiatives are up and running and have shown they can get some manner of results. Sometimes other donors or partners can fill the gap, but not always, and possibly not even most of the time. When that is the case, the consequences and risks of exiting are often immediate and direct, particularly for the people or issues that are benefitting from those programs and can least afford to lose them.

The lesson here isn't that once you make a commitment to an organization you have to sustain it indefinitely. It is to be mindful of the impact your philanthropy will have on the recipients, and to do your best not to create unintended consequences that forethought might have forestalled (in the case above, for example, by thinking explicitly about your exit as well as your entrance).

Unlike the strategic risk of wasting your resources, secondary risks are borne entirely by others and can therefore be quite easy to undervalue. Your philanthropy may "succeed," but if it does so at a significant cost to others, your net benefit to society may actually be negative. Avoiding all risk is impossible; considering the risk that others will bear as equal in importance to the risks you yourself are willing to embrace is not.

The last form of risk, *personal risk*, is the risk of disappointment or embarrassment: the risk that at the end of the day, your philanthropy fails to bring you real satisfaction or, worse, that it compromises your reputation. Because failure is always disappointing (and a failed initiative may cast a cloud over anyone closely associated with it), there is an obvious overlap between strategic risk and personal risk. But personal risk also has personal roots; in particular, the shortfall in being altogether clear about your own motivations, desires, and needs.

The best way to manage personal risk is to confront the hard questions that no one else will ask you, and to be ruthlessly honest with yourself in answering them. Questions like "If I knew that I would never receive public recognition for the success I've helped to realize, would I still want to get involved in this initiative?" Or "To what extent am I willing to risk aspects of my reputation to achieve success?" Or "Do I really care enough about this issue to take satisfaction in its achievement, even if it turns out to require substantially more money and time than I anticipated having to commit?"

Candid answers to questions like these will not only help you avoid personal disappointment, but also give you the last piece of information you need to decide whether the results you're aiming for, and the resources you're able and willing to commit, are sufficiently aligned to move forward. If the honest answer is "not really," now is the time to double back to your definition of success and your theory of change—instead of plunging in and discovering, too late, that you've fallen prey to an excess of blind confidence.

Philanthropists by and large are a confident breed, and rightly so. They are confident in their capabilities to make things happen, confident in their insights and judgment, and accustomed to thinking big and aiming high. As a result, they are often unafraid to target society's toughest problems, or to seek out new approaches to those problems. And without a doubt, such self-confidence can be an enormous asset and a strong engine for impact, particularly given philanthropy's freedom to experiment and take risks that other institutions cannot.

But when confidence is combined with a passion for social change and a disinclination to be ruthlessly realistic about what success will actually require, it can also be a philanthropist's undoing. As a cautionary tale, consider what happened to one prominent national funder that wanted to start a new program to solve child poverty in America's most blighted cities.

With some $5–$10 million per year, the foundation's leaders knew they didn't have enough money to make a meaningful difference in a large urban center like New York or Los Angeles. So they took what they thought was the right step, and looked for mid-sized cities, where there were 50,000 to 100,000 poor children for whom their dollars could have a transformative effect.

Unfortunately, the foundation's leadership fell in love with their strategy before making sure it was plausible. In fact, they were so excited that they began holding meetings in one of the cities. They dreamed big with local funders, community leaders, and potential nonprofit grantees, thereby sending everyone's expectations through the roof.

At the same time, however, an analysis of urban antipoverty efforts spelled out in stark detail what it would actually take to make a meaningful difference in the lives of children in a given locale: a deep understanding of the community (which this foundation did not have); a high degree of readiness on the part of local entities, and state and city agencies to embrace an outside funder with no ties to the community; a commitment to invest for the long haul; and a willingness to forego simplistic metrics in favor of more complex indicators of a community's health.

Unfortunately, this funder met none of the requirements. Nor, as it turned out, did it have nearly enough money: the $5–$10 million they were prepared to spend would be insufficient to temporarily feed the city's children, let alone tackle the other poverty-induced problems they faced.

EXCELLENCE IS SELF-IMPOSED

Of all the characteristics that distinguish philanthropists, the single most consequential may be the fact that they are essentially accountable to no one but themselves.

Sooner or later, businesspeople, politicians, and nonprofit leaders all have to answer for their performance to others: business executives to their stakeholders; politicians to the electorate; nonprofit leaders to their funders. Philanthropists have no such "market" dynamics with which to contend. On the contrary! The world they inhabit is a cross between the Galapagos Islands and the mythical Lake Wobegon: there is a blissful absence of predators, and all of the children are above average.

If you doubt this, consider just a few of the most telling differences between the world of philanthropy and the world of business, the realm from which so many leading philanthropists, past and present, have come.

Business executives are accountable to their stakeholders for delivering short- and long-term results of every kind: financial results (such as revenue growth, return on investment and earnings per share); strategic results (such as customer loyalty and market share); and operating results (such as cost margins and employee retention). Those who "make their numbers" are rewarded; those who continually fall short are replaced. None can hide for long from the facts of their performance.

Nor can they escape feedback from the marketplace. If customers become dissatisfied, those customers defect. If talented employees become disaffected, they decamp. If competitors introduce more innovative products and services, they grab market share. Data on sales is timely, precise, and irrefutable. Winning and losing have a direct impact on the company, as well as on its executives. The invisible hand of the market drives toward continuous improvement, whether individuals want to learn and improve, or not.

In philanthropy, none of these dynamics exists. With a handful of exceptions (such as community foundations, which must raise money from donors every year, and compete for those donors with private wealth managers), philanthropists have no customers, no competitors, and no markets to confront them with any harsh realities. The only externally imposed requirements for foundations are to maintain a "reasonable" cost structure, and to pay out at least 5 percent of their assets on philanthropic activities (including some administrative expenses) each year. Individual philanthropists, who choose to operate through donor-advised funds or simply their own checkbooks, are free from even these minimal constraints.

Feedback, too, is scant, and what there is tends to be suspect. When you're in the business of giving away money, people tend to tell you what they think you want to hear. A smart, self-confident, accomplished person awash in reassuring rhetoric can easily fall victim to self-deception, and to believing that his or her philanthropy is having far more impact than it actually is.

What is the inescapable conclusion? Simply this: if you are truly committed to achieving as much impact as is practical with your limited philanthropic resources, you will have to demand excellence of yourself. And that means being willing to engage in the hard work of setting a high bar, and holding yourself accountable for clearing it.

Pursuing outstanding results, year after year, when they are not being demanded by anyone else is not a natural act. It takes extraordinary determination and self-discipline. Such behavior is like striving for straight As in a school without grades, or exercising aggressively day after day, simply because it is the right thing to do. And it is especially difficult in the absence of robust data. Imagine working your heart out to achieve all those As, then receiving a report card that reads: "Incomplete: Inadequate Information."

In philanthropy, where results can be extremely difficult to measure, impact may take years or even decades to achieve, and the direct consequences of your particular contribution may be impossible to determine. Such circumstances easily erode motivation.

Self-imposed accountability is also "unnatural," in the sense that if you set a high bar, you may not clear it, and that can be embarrassing, particularly in a world that largely shuns failure. So if no one is demanding that you set a high standard and hold yourself accountable for meeting it, and if doing so is hard (and risks embarrassment), why ever would you do it?

The answer, in a word, is "impact"—and your commitment to making changes for the better on society's behalf. In philanthropy, as in every other human endeavor, excellence doesn't "just happen." It takes resolve, perseverance, and the disciplined pursuit of high performance. That, in turn, requires excellent execution, on your part and on the part of the organizations and individuals to whom you provide resources, and on whose performance your own ability to create results will in large measure depend. That is the topic to which we now turn.

4

WHAT WILL IT TAKE TO GET THE JOB DONE?

YOU'VE GOTTEN CLEAR ABOUT THE SUCCESS you want to see, and about the results for which you intend to hold yourself accountable. Now the overarching question becomes, *"What will it take to get the job done?"*

This question marks a turning point, both in the journey from aspirations to impact and in the focus of our narrative. It is the point at which the emphasis shifts from designing to doing; that is, to execution. Execution is where strategy becomes real and where your best thinking gets tested. It is also where the learning that informs strategy, and leads to better results over time, happens—or doesn't happen.

The most elegant strategy is useless if it can't be implemented effectively. This is true whether the strategy in question is designed to create a new business, develop a world-class sports team, or help homeless young people move off the streets and stay off the streets. Lofty aspirations and intriguing theories of change have the power to capture our imaginations, inspire us, and win our initial commitment. But in the end, results on the ground require disciplined blocking and tackling, complemented by the capacity to learn and improve over time.

In this chapter, we'll focus on the organizational capacity required for effective execution. Thousands of books and articles have been written about organizational effectiveness. (Amazon alone lists more than three thousand such volumes.) And yet the essential elements are straightforward: right people, right processes, and right costs. In order to deliver and sustain outstanding results, you need to employ the right people in the right jobs, develop processes that enable those individuals to work together to make smart decisions, and provide them with appropriate resources through a sustainable financial model.

Getting this right is easier said than done. But as a philanthropist, you face special challenges because your ability to achieve results will largely depend on the performance of the nonprofit and nongovernmental organizations you choose to support. So in addition to thinking about the capacity you will need to carry out your own philanthropic activities, you also have to think about the capacity of the grantees who will bear the brunt of the responsibility for doing the work and delivering results. We will look at the challenges of effective execution for both donors and their grantees shortly. First, however, we'll seek inspiration in Boston, where effective execution is turning an innovative strategy into real gains for the community.

JOHN SIMON:
ADOPTING AND ADAPTING NEW IDEAS

John Simon, managing director of General Catalyst Partners, has always been interested in social action and direct service to communities in need.[1] As an undergraduate at Harvard, he volunteered with the Massachusetts Special Olympics. Later, he went to Oxford as a Rhodes Scholar and, discovering that there was no equivalent to the Special Olympics program in England, helped begin a modest effort called KEEN (Kids Enjoy Exercise Now) to teach tennis to kids with disabilities. KEEN quickly took off, spreading to two other United Kingdom cities and, eventually, eight cities in the United States. The work itself was immensely rewarding, Simon recalls, but he also found himself equally excited by the idea that a powerful philanthropic concept could "replicate" itself.

When he returned to Boston in 1988, Simon went into the private equity business, but the itch to serve society persisted. So Simon and his roommate, a friend from Oxford named Michael P. Danziger, then about to graduate from the Harvard Graduate School of Education, began looking for another good idea to adopt and, perhaps, adapt. They focused on a New York City–based program called Prep for Prep, which provided tutoring to late-elementary- and early-middle-school-aged kids to help them get admitted to the city's elite private schools. In 1990, with encouragement from Prep for Prep's founder, Gary Simons, Simon and Danziger set up the Boston-based Steppingstone Foundation, which faithfully reproduced many of the elements of the successful New York program. The new program soon showed positive results, and Simon and Danziger began looking for ways to expand the concept to additional cities. They established the first spin-off in Philadelphia in 1998.

But, of course, it wasn't as simple as hanging out a Steppingstone shingle and turning on the lights in a new city. It took five years before the Philadelphia program was able to match

Boston's performance, and by then cracks were beginning to show in the larger operation. "We started to notice that we were outrunning our supply lines," Simon recalls. "In the for-profit world, if your business model is good enough, you can expand and get stronger. In the not-for-profit world, you get weaker, because your fundraising base is local. So it became clear that this beautiful model was not going to get to other cities easily."

What to do? From the experience with Steppingstone, Simon realized that any city trying to import an idea needed a large number of supports. Executing to a high standard required not just a great model, but also a great many other things: the right people, in the form of an executive director and a strong board; the right processes, including assessing local needs, adapting the model to meet them, and building a local coalition of supporters; and the right financial model, including sufficient funding to support the program for its first few difficult start-up years.

"That started to crystallize in my mind the idea of a systematic 'idea importer,'" Simon recalls. The importer would help shoulder the huge burdens of execution by fund-raising, finding leadership, and providing local insights, thereby enabling more and better replication of programs that had been shown to work. "If a city had one of those," he hypothesized, "it could change in a quantum leap, over a period of years. And what if that organization then replicated itself across many cities? That could revolutionize the whole way that nonprofit ideas spread."

By 2003, Simon was ready to launch the GreenLight Fund to help bring nonprofits with strong results to new cities. And, of course, Simon faced the same execution challenges in starting GreenLight as did the nonprofits around him. Searching for the right person to lead the organization, he quickly identified Margaret Hall. With extensive experience in nonprofit capacity building and philanthropy, she brought valuable social sector expertise to the new endeavor.

Working as cofounders, Hall and Simon developed the right processes, starting with a rigorous due diligence process involving many local experts who could help them accurately gauge the city's needs and evaluate programs elsewhere that might meet them. Because their vision included expanding GreenLight to other cities, even the decision to start in Boston was intentional. Boston has a reputation for being something of a "not-invented-here" city. So "if you could do it here," Simon explains, "you could probably do it in hundreds of cities across the U.S., and across the world."

They also thought hard, and creatively, about the cost part of the equation. In addition to significant guidance from Hall and local advisors, the new nonprofits they were bringing to the city would likely require at least four or five years of financial help, as they built up a base of local support. That meant GreenLight had to develop a strong core of funders who would accept an unlikely proposition: bet on our next great idea. "Our model requires that donors sign up to support this year's GreenLight thing without even knowing what it will be," says Simon. The donors, many of whom are active in private equity or high-tech businesses, trust GreenLight's leaders, rigorous due diligence, and track record of results. By bringing together the right people and processes, Green-Light has been able to fund the right costs.

As of this writing, GreenLight has brought five programs to Boston in its first six years, each meeting a specific community need. For example, Friends of the Children seeks to break the cycle of poverty by providing stable mentoring relationships with caring adults for high-risk youth. Raising a Reader promotes early literacy and reading readiness by helping families establish enjoyable routines for reading together.

So far, GreenLight is achieving its desired results: the new nonprofits have successfully matched, or surpassed, their founding organizations' programmatic results. As important, they have been transitioning away from GreenLight's support and demonstrating growing strength to thrive independently. The next phase, Simon anticipates, will be the replication of GreenLight itself. He and Hall have taken preliminary steps in that direction by seeking funding to support such an effort. They've also put the word out: "Feel free to borrow this idea."

"If a John equivalent and a Margaret equivalent popped up in, say, Denver," Simon concludes, "and came to us and said, 'We want to learn everything there is to know about GreenLight and replicate it,' we would be very interested."

WHAT'S THE RIGHT CAPACITY FOR MY PHILANTHROPY?

The "right" capacity is a function of the strategy you're pursuing, and the results you're holding yourself accountable for. As you think about what you need to get the job done, you will probably find that you've already answered at least a few of the relevant questions by defining the role that you, personally, want to play in your philanthropy. The time and resources you are willing to commit, and the level of personal engagement you desire, all have implications for what portion of the execution you will want to shoulder. In some cases, you may not need much (if any) additional capacity; for instance, if you are giving money to an organization you know well and where you volunteer or serve on the board.

Underscoring that point, there is no law that says you have to create a foundation to be a philanthropist, even if you are regularly giving away very large sums of money. One of the most significant contributors to environmental causes we know had no formal organization whatsoever until recently, when he hired an assistant to help in the preliminary research and "tire-kicking" related to prospective new grants. There are many other philanthropists like him, who choose to manage their giving entirely on their own, through a donor-advised fund at a community foundation, or with the aid of a philanthropic consultant, or through a family office that manages both their investments and their charitable contributions.

Once you formally involve even one person beyond yourself in your decision-making process (in the form of paid staff or volunteer board members), however, you've taken the first step toward creating an organization. This means that, sooner or later, you will have to think about whether you have the essential elements of an effective organization in place. And because so much of the work of philanthropy ultimately comes down to people making decisions about the use of resources—their time, expertise, and energy, and your money—you will have to get really clear about what the key decisions are, who has the authority to make them, and where you intend to inject yourself into the process.

This all sounds very straightforward when it's couched in the rational, impersonal language of management, as we've done above. But the truth is that philanthropy is rarely rational and dispassionate (and almost never so in a family context). So as you're thinking through these issues, it's helpful to anticipate the most common pitfalls, keep your eyes open for them, and confront them directly when they appear—as they almost certainly will.

FIRST "WHO"

The first law of effective organizations, as Jim Collins[2] and others point out, is having the right people in the right jobs at the right time. In philanthropy, finding the "right" people is often challenging. The skills required span multiple fields, and the supply of potential candidates with deep, relevant experience and demonstrated track records is comparatively small. Unlike in business, there are relatively few opportunities to hire a proven foundation CEO, recruit an accomplished senior program executive, or promote an up-and-comer from within. This is especially true for younger and smaller foundations.

As for the requisite skill set, consider the criteria against which a candidate to head up a family foundation might reasonably be evaluated:

- Personal fit with the donor, and perhaps the donor's family
- Previous experience as a grant maker
- Experience in the field or program area in which the foundation will work
- General management ability

- Nonprofit experience, which will be relevant to grantees
- Personal attributes such as integrity, intelligence, reputation, and energy

The longer the list gets, the less likely it is that anyone except a deity or superhero could possibly fit the bill. In fact, after many years in and around the field of philanthropy, we have yet to meet a "perfect" candidate—the man or woman who could score well along all these dimensions. So, realistically, the question is, given your particular circumstances, which of these attributes are essential, and where are you willing to make compromises?

Many donors conclude that firsthand knowledge of the person's character and competence (often established through a preexisting relationship, and characterized as "personal fit") is the primary criterion. Pierre Omidyar, for example, ultimately recruited a former eBay colleague, Matt Bannick, to lead the Omidyar Network. Herb and Marion Sandler tapped their longtime attorney to run their foundation.

Others prioritize field expertise and specialized skills. John Simon valued Margaret Hall's deep knowledge of the social sector, in addition to the management skills and charisma needed for GreenLight Fund's start-up phase. When the Gates Foundation sought to advance its education strategy, it chose Vicki Phillips, who was then serving as the superintendent of Portland Public Schools and had a long track record of successful involvement in school reform, at both the state and local levels, to lead the initiative.

Making trade-offs around qualifications is best accomplished when you are crystal clear about the actual job that

YOUR FIRST HIRE

Your first hire represents a new stage in your philanthropy, and sets it in a new direction. It is, simply, the most important staffing decision you will make. What can help you get it right?

First, trust is the single most important criterion. All philanthropy is personal, not just for you and your family, but also for your staff. A lawyer or wealth manager need not share your passions to give you good advice about your legal or investment decisions, but that's not the case with the person who will help you give away your money. Whether you are envisioning your new hire as a strategic thought partner, or expect him or her to play a more execution-oriented role, that person's values and beliefs need to be strongly aligned with yours. Otherwise, you risk ending up in a messy and inevitably unproductive tangle.

Trust, in the context of a donor-staff member relationship, is a complex mix of shared values, mutual respect, and personal chemistry. That doesn't mean you should hire a friend, a situation that creates its own complications. It does mean hiring someone whose professional competence you respect, and who you think will help you make better decisions over time.

Second, you need to think hard, not only about whether you want a partner or a strong right hand, but also whether you need a generalist or

needs to be done, and—emphatically—the role that you personally (and perhaps your family members) expect to play. A headhunter can draft a job description in an hour, but it will be a useless exercise unless you first have been brutally honest about your own assumptions and intentions. If you expect to be actively involved in all the most important decisions, then you may actually need a chief operating officer rather than a a specialist. If you know you're passionate about supporting emerging artists, for example, you might choose someone who is an artist herself, or who has worked in (or even run) a museum or gallery. The set of skills and experiences such a specialist would bring can greatly inform your decision making. The risk with a specialist is that since she will also bring her own point of view (that is, after all, one of the reasons you'd hire her), she may urge you to make choices that do not exactly line up with your own point of view.

Conversely, if you have not yet completely defined your priorities and are still experimenting with different types of philanthropy and causes to support, you might choose a generalist as your first hire. A generalist is less likely to have a stake in one particular approach, and more likely to be open and helpful in advising you as your priorities evolve. However, you may want to supplement his or her work by contracting with specialists who can provide expert insights into how to generate results in particular fields without also driving your decision making.

Finally, think about how long you want your first hire to be in his or her role. Whatever form this position takes, it isn't likely to last forever. So it's probably wise to be clear from the outset that you expect your staff needs to shift as your philanthropy evolves.

CEO. True, you might have better luck attracting top applicants with the bigger title. But you would risk setting yourself up for future conflict, which in turn would risk reducing the potential impact of your philanthropy (and create unnecessary headaches).

If you doubt this could happen as the result of a single bad hire, consider the following cautionary tale.

"WRONG WHO"

The foundation launched with several hundred million dollars in assets. Its benefactor, having sold his company, had decided to devote his considerable energy, extensive network, and burgeoning financial resources to curing a disease that had plagued his family in recent generations. At an advanced age, he did not have time on his side. He needed to move fast, scale his organization, and get money out the door. His daughter agreed to be involved in the new foundation part time, hoping to balance the job with her family responsibilities. But what the philanthropist really needed, or so he thought, was a top-notch CEO—someone aggressive and smart, with national stature, who could make the right things happen fast.

After a dozen phone calls, the philanthropist decided that he had found his man. We'll call him "Walter Connors." Walter was a medical doctor, a brilliant researcher, a former hospital chief—his resume seemed to have it all. The philanthropist had met Connors several times over the years and liked what he saw. After a lengthy dinner, culminating in an exceptionally generous offer, Connors signed on and entered the world of family philanthropy.

Less than a year later, the foundation had a well-appointed office and a staff of eight truly outstanding young people in addition to Connors. Money was flowing, press releases had been issued, Connors was in great demand as a keynote speaker at conferences. To all appearances, it was a brilliant start-up.

In fact, it was an unmitigated mess. Much to the dismay of the benefactor, Connors was making unilateral decisions, amplifying his already high profile, and behaving as if he were giving away his *own* money. Although he was conducting himself as if he were an accomplished CEO, in fact he was proving to be a terrible manager, making mediocre decisions punctuated by seemingly random commitments. Personal communication between him and his "boss" had broken down. Their conversations, once frequent and stimulating for both men, were now sporadic and awkward. The philanthropist was thoroughly uncomfortable about the prospect of confronting his trophy CEO. For his part, Connors—fully absorbed in his exciting new crusade—ignored the gathering storm.

Meanwhile, the benefactor's daughter had been pulled into the foundation full time, in a convoluted role as "head of all programs." She reported to both her father and the CEO, and was almost boiling over with frustration. Soon the other employees were openly discussing the chaos around them, and the best among them were actively job hunting. The internal tumult was having a predictable effect on current and potential grantees, all of whom found it nearly impossible to interact productively with the foundation. Phone calls went unanswered, grant requests had to be rewritten repeatedly, and tentative agreements were being reneged upon.

One year later, the philanthropist hit the reset button. He abruptly fired Connors and put his daughter in charge. It was a humiliating episode for all concerned, but especially for the well-meaning benefactor. What he had viewed as the capstone of an illustrious career had degenerated into a debacle. It had cost him valuable time and money. It had damaged his personal reputation, as well as the reputation and effectiveness of the foundation.

Given how many contemporary philanthropists are business executives with a proven eye for talent, it is remarkable how often they end up hiring the "wrong who" for key foundation leadership roles. We select the people we think we know, rather than the people we actually need. Becoming star-struck with a celebrity who has an outstanding resume (as happened above) is an all too common trap. Another is hiring a friend from one's prior life (perhaps a faithful junior executive or business associate) who is a known quantity, but is not well suited to the demands of a totally different kind of activity. Putting spouses or offspring in key positions at a family foundation can create other complex dynamics, even in cases where those family members are highly competent and actually *want* to serve in those positions.

WHICH COMES FIRST, THE STRATEGY OR THE PEOPLE?

In an ideal world, your strategy would be fully developed and your future role would be perfectly clear before you'd need to make any capacity decisions. But life is rarely that orderly. For example, your strategy may be premised on many as yet unanswered questions in your theory of change. You may not know exactly how your role will evolve, or how much time you and your spouse will ultimately spend in this work. (And, of course, whatever you decide now is likely to change over time as your circumstances shift.) There may also be at least a few people in place already, particularly if your philanthropy has been institutionalized in a foundation.

So which comes first, the strategy or the people? There is no single prescription, other than to proceed with caution, in an iterative manner. One foundation, which started recently, hired its first president for a single three-year term to help design the strategy and jump-start the organization. Once that work is accomplished, he will be replaced by a permanent hire—someone who, in the eyes of both the donor and the temporary president, will be a good fit with the foundation's strategy.

Questions about whether people or strategy come first can also crop up within established institutions, especially those venturing into a new arena. Here's a case in point. Shocked by the rising incidence of substance abuse among young people, a well-endowed foundation brought in a new senior program officer who had decades of experience working on the issue. Not surprisingly, she had strong ideas about where she wanted to take the program, and believed she had the mandate and authority to chart its course. Within months, though, it became apparent that the benefactor had a different (and equally plausible) direction in mind. Many hours of discussion and debate followed, to no avail. Two years later, the program officer was asked to leave, never having grasped the basic fact that the two strategies—hers and the foundation's—were at odds.

This unhappy scenario was unusual not because of the hiring mistake, but because it was addressed swiftly. In philanthropy, and especially in a foundation setting, the far more common outcome is to cobble together a "compromise," in the name of consensus, that allows the individual to pursue some aspects of his or her desired direction. The problem with this "solution" is that it dilutes the strategy—and of course the available resources—and thereby undermines the foundation's potential to achieve results.

Perhaps you're wondering about the statement that two years constituted a swift amount of time for resolution. In philanthropy, as in the nonprofit sector generally, replacing people tends to be disproportionately difficult. Two years was indeed "speedy."

Many factors contribute to this problem, including the absence of clear performance metrics, inconsistent performance review practices, cultural norms that stress that "we're all in this together," the inherent disruption of replacing people, and the challenge of recruiting talented people. Giving in to these obstacles won't solve anything, however, if the person was the wrong hire in the first place, or if what is required to do the job well has changed.

In philanthropy, as in other walks of life, you need to keep in mind the "right time" corollary of the "right people, right job" principle, because job requirements and individuals are both dynamic: A leader who is extraordinarily well suited to a foundation start-up may not be a natural fit to run it as it becomes a large, established institution. A senior program officer accustomed to making the key decisions in his area of expertise is unlikely to be satisfied if the locus of decision making shifts in response to a new strategic direction within the foundation.

Smaller foundations (which are the vast majority of all foundations) have their own challenges. Because career paths tend to be limited, individuals can easily linger too long in the same position, hurting both themselves and the organization. While "bad turnover" (losing a star program officer because she is burned out, for example) is obviously undesirable, good turnover is necessary, both to refresh the organization and to help people refresh themselves.

DOES YOUR BOARD "GIVE SMART"?

If you are a donor with a family foundation, a trustee serving on a foundation board, or a foundation executive interfacing with a board, you already know full well that a board's performance can greatly enhance—or dramatically cripple—your ability to deliver results. Foundation boards are typically accountable for fundamental decisions ranging from strategic direction and resource allocation to staff recruiting and grant approval. If those decisions are not made wisely, you cannot achieve the success you hope for.

Effective board-level decision making can be elusive, however, especially in family foundations. When these institutions work well, they provide powerful testimony to the enduring values of individual families. But the combination of donor, spouse, and adult children (including, perhaps, their spouses) creates a group often better suited for holiday gatherings than serious decision making. Add in a couple of independent trustees to contribute balance and expertise (along with their own agendas), and you can have quite a volatile concoction, with people importing family dynamics that may have evolved over decades, personal passions, and (often strident) points of view into every board meeting.

Moreover, unlike privately held family businesses, philanthropic boards have no performance metrics or profit motive to defuse these dynamics and help their members align around common goals. If anything, the deeply personal nature of philanthropy can drive the dynamics in exactly the opposite direction. And in foundations established in perpetuity, where the board must have the ability to sustain and renew itself across generations, this tumult is often intensified. How are new board members chosen? Who serves as chair? Do trustees have terms, or are they appointed for life? What is the appropriate mix of family members versus independent trustees? And are all trustees equal when it comes to decision making?

Given such tensions, it's not surprising that foundation boards often lack clarity of purpose. Is the board's primary purpose to provide legal oversight and compliance with good governance practices? Is the real (if unstated) purpose to serve the family, by creating a forum for collaboration, learning, and public service? Or is the board truly accountable to society for adding value in a way that ultimately increases philanthropic results?

These competing imperatives have very different implications, and achieving excellence on all three dimensions can be frustratingly complex. You cannot, for example, perpetually please every family member and, at the same time, make the tough trade-offs inherent in pursuing an effective strategy. Similarly, the time commitment, board structures, and procedures required by basic governance practices (such as financial and strategic performance monitoring, and the board nomination process) can severely circumscribe the time available for the higher-yield thinking that adds real value to a strategy.

We believe that good governance is necessary but not sufficient; that a foundation exists to serve society, not itself and its trustees. Consequently, boards must be designed and led in a manner that produces the best possible results, given the available resources. That's why the "right people, right jobs, right time" principle is as apt and relevant here as it is for staff, although the constraints on enacting it are typically far greater. (It is usually not very easy to choose one child over another to serve as a trustee, for example.)

Even with the "right" trustees, you will need a decision-making process that yields objective, thoughtful decisions. And you will need to be vigilant about maintaining its integrity in the face of some very natural inclinations: to allow family or personal interests to upstage strategic imperatives; to permit opinion unwittingly to substitute for fact; and, in a quest for consensus (and family harmony), to sidestep the hard choices necessary to develop and execute effective strategies.

Foundations that employ professional staff, whether the number is one or one hundred, often encounter significant problems with the board-staff interface. These problems come in many varieties, from confusion and conflict about how decisions are made, to unproductive working relationships with the foundation's CEO, to excessive and unnecessary burdens placed on the staff by individual trustees.

A foundation is like a luxury automobile, headed in a specific, mission-driven direction, with a clear road map on the GPS. The car is "owned" by the board, but mostly driven by the staff, who work full time, while the board members visit occasionally. During those visits, however, trustees naturally tend to slide into the front seat and grab the steering wheel. And although they appreciate how clean and shiny the car is (because the staff has stayed up all night polishing the chrome), they can often fail to read the owner's manual (written by the staff). Trustees, quite naturally, feel that they are running the foundation; staff, quite naturally, feel that key decisions are largely theirs to make. As a result, their interactions, however well intentioned, can be laced with flawed communications, wasted time and energy, and dysfunctional decision making that compromises results.

GETTING DECISION MAKING RIGHT

The capacity to make and implement smart decisions is a defining feature of an effective organization. In philanthropy, this capacity is also the engine for driving impact. Clarity around who is accountable for which decisions can lead to more effective, efficient, and responsive decisions, greater transparency, and reduced conflict—all of which not only improve life for the people making the decisions, but also make it far easier for their grantees to engage with them and get on with their own important work.

Ambiguity has precisely the opposite effect, both internally and externally. Poor decision making is one of the most serious ways in which funders undermine the effectiveness of their grantees. Unfortunately, it is also remarkably common.

Dysfunctional decision making isn't limited to philanthropic institutions, of course, but they often exhibit its symptoms in dramatic ways. As noted above, this tends to be particularly true in family foundations. Families are neither rational nor professional, and as a group they seldom make results-focused decisions the way a high-performing company board or executive team would. Even spouses who have been married for decades may find it challenging to work together giving money away. So it's not surprising that agreement and forward motion can get stalled, especially when the decision makers represent multiple generations and very different points of view.

Even when family dynamics aren't part of the mix, decision rights and responsibilities can get tangled over time. One long-established foundation had both a well-articulated set of strategies spanning four distinct program areas and a clearly delineated process for making grants. Program directors were authorized to commit sums up to $100,000 unilaterally for any single grant in their area. Grants of $500,000 required the approval of the CEO, and grants above $1 million went to the board of trustees.

These policies had been in place for many years, and seemed eminently sensible to everyone involved. But what looked good on paper wasn't working in reality. A careful analysis showed that almost 90 percent of all grants—and the vast majority of annual funding—were commitments of just a shade less than $100,000, and the number of such grants had grown dramatically over the past ten years. In addition, these single-year commitments had an 85 percent renewal rate. As a result, decision making had devolved from the foundation's leadership to the lowest level of its staff, the opposite of what the policies intended.

Had this shift been an explicit imperative—had the foundation's leaders decided to empower the frontline in a way consistent with a theory of change—this could have been a fine outcome. But, in reality, this behavior had literally nothing to do with the foundation's strategy. It had come about so gradually that the organization was utterly unaware of the change. It was the result of professionals pursuing their passions and agendas in their own program silos, which had simply led to further drift.

Achieving results demands clarity about how decisions are made, and the discipline to make them within the context of your theory of change. This usually means saying no most of the time, both to avoid making grants that would throw your strategy off course, and so that you can "double down" when that is desirable from a strategic perspective.

It also means being honest and clear about who gets to decide what. If a board of trustees is responsible for approving every grant and has a 99 percent approval rate, it's reasonable to infer that the board's decision-making role is mainly a formality. But if a benefactor can override any decisions made by staff, and does so on a regular basis, then perhaps decision-making authority needs to be structured accordingly.

Similarly, if family members exercise direct control over certain programs, to the point of shaping grants and bypassing the foundation's CEO, then perhaps that decision-making loop should be acknowledged. Or if the cornerstone of decision making is consensus within the foundation's executive team, then perhaps the details of the "consensus" should be explicitly defined. Although none of these processes is inherently bad, it is damaging to espouse one process while implementing a very different one. Good people get frustrated, results are diminished, and the odds of making poor decisions multiply.

Decision processes are messy and imperfect in every organization. People lobby behind the scenes. Politics comes into play, and personal power is exercised. But if results are your goal, you can't allow the confusion—or disarray around accountability for decisions—to persist. You can have exceptions to the rules. But make them conscious exceptions, so that you can determine how your decisions are compounding over time, either for good or for ill.

ARE YOU COST CONSCIOUS, OR UNCONSCIOUSLY CONSTRAINED?

At a recent board meeting of a foundation that receives donations from the public, the executive director, a highly sophisticated and acclaimed individual, announced proudly that "our overhead costs are less than five percent of annual giving."[3] This statement was met with approving nods from the esteemed group around the table, including the primary benefactor. The message in both directions was clear: overhead is bad, and cutting overhead to the bone is good. But in the quest for results is 5 percent a worthy accomplishment, or is it a problem in disguise? If 5 percent is laudable, is 4 percent automatically better? How about 2 percent? If "less is always best" when it comes to overhead, should the benefactor dispense with the foundation altogether and just write personal checks?

In any philanthropic situation, the best level and mix of costs is the one required to get the job done, consistent with the donor's or foundation's accountability, theory of change, and desired results. In other words, the right cost structure is one that is customized to your particular goals and strategy. A Fortune 500 business would never benchmark itself against all other Fortune 500 corporations. Averaging hundreds of companies across dozens of industries and strategies would be a useless exercise. Worse still, it would amount to benchmarking oneself not against the highest-performing organizations, but against an array of companies collectively generating average results. Yet this is exactly the kind of thing that happens when otherwise sensible foundation donors and trustees assert that "we should limit our costs to 15 percent (pick a number) of total grant making." Or "We've benchmarked ourselves against the top twenty-five foundations and, great news, we are low cost!" Or "We must reduce our total overhead; otherwise, we're wasting our money!"

These are right instincts, wrongly applied.

There are two kinds of overhead: good and bad. Like all organizations, foundations have to keep a sharp eye on their cost structure, and some expenditures (lavish offices, for instance, and surplus secretarial support) are certainly prime suspects in the "bad" overhead category. But there is no such thing as a free lunch. If you want to establish the operational capacity to achieve great results, you will have to pay what it takes to hire top-notch staff. Conversely, if you pinch pennies and recruit "B" players, your upside will be constrained. There is no avoiding the fact that both your strategy and your ability to execute it are inexorably tied to your cost structure. The key is to focus more on the *value* that the costs generate than on the costs themselves.

Adding internal capacity adds cost. Whether that cost is productive will depend on whether it actually enables you and/or your grantees to achieve better results consistent with your strategy. If you are making multimillion-dollar investments in a small number of nonprofit service providers, the way the Edna McConnell Clark Foundation does, you had better be excellent at due diligence and supporting grantees. If you are trying to influence public will and public policy, as the Irvine Foundation is, you had best hire people with policy experience and superb communications skills. If you're creating and disseminating knowledge, you need to make sure that your organization is designed around, and plugged into, all the networks of experts who are relevant in and for your field.

As this last example suggests, you may not need to employ all the people you require to get the job done. Decades ago, if you wanted something done well, it was probably best to do it yourself. Today, a variety of enabling conditions—ranging from technology, to ever more specialized service providers, to globalization—have dramatically altered that dynamic. "Outsourcing" important parts of your work has the potential to improve quality, lower costs, and enhance results in philanthropy, just as it does in business. You might hire external organizations that specialize in communications, or seek expert advisors and reviewers to manage and assess your grants. The Robert Wood Johnson Foundation, for example, contracts with professionals across the country (primarily university-based scholars and administrators) to run its national programs.

As you consider your own philanthropic capacity, the challenge is to avoid both overreaching and underreaching. Many of today's self-made philanthropists are accustomed to thinking and acting successfully on a very large canvas. The temptation to think you can do it all yourself can be very strong—and lead to more organization building than your strategy actually warrants. On the other hand, many foundation leaders underestimate the potential they actually have to help their grantees by leveraging the organization's reputation and contacts: introducing them to other potential donors who are part of their own networks, for example, or organizing a critical meeting with local officials that a nonprofit leader could never have pulled off alone. To strike the right balance, you need to understand what you uniquely are capable of doing, and put that capacity fully to work for the benefit of your grantees.

WHAT DO GRANTEES REALLY NEED
TO GET THE JOB DONE?

Identifying the capacity you need to implement your philanthropic strategy is the first step in answering the question, "What will it take to get the job done?" The second, and in many respects more difficult, step is identifying nonprofit organizations or NGOs with the capacity to take on the downstream half of getting the job done; namely, doing the work successfully on the ground. To repeat what we said at the beginning of this chapter, in most cases your philanthropy will largely be defined by the performance of your grantees. So whatever decisions you ultimately make about your own capacity, the capacity to select well is a "must have."

We will take up the topic of grantee selection in the next chapter, as part of a larger discussion of effective grant-making processes and practices. To set the stage for that discussion, however, the last few pages of this chapter are devoted to the issue of organizational capacity in the nonprofit sector and, more specifically, what some of the common problems and shortfalls are. This knowledge is indispensible not only to choosing the right grantees, but also to guiding your thinking about how to fund and support the organizations you ultimately select.

Built to break. Like you, your grantees need the right capacity to deliver the results you and they expect to see. Practically speaking, this means they need the leadership and management to sustain good performance, the right processes and systems to manage their programs and operations, and the funding to support their activities. You'll recognize the formula: right people, right processes, and right costs.

Unfortunately, the facts of life in the social sector make all three of these dimensions problematic for nonprofits. We'll start with leadership and management, the "right people" part of the equation.

Put simply, many nonprofits are strongly led but under-managed.[4] The leaders of these organizations are often genuinely inspirational figures, passionate about their work and, in many cases, driven to extend their positive influence into adjacent realms. Their power to set compelling visions, motivate followers, and build cohesive cultures is amazing. They tend to fall short, however, when it comes to critical management activities, such as translating their visions into clear organizational priorities, providing employees with performance feedback and developing future leaders, and defining clear decision-making roles.[5]

Why the imbalance? For one, nonprofit leaders typically come from the fields in which their organizations are engaged: community development, for example, or child welfare. Their resumes usually don't include management experience in organizations other than their own. And the environment in which they work reinforces visionary leadership at the expense of management discipline. Passion, coupled with the ability to make a compelling case for a cause, drives fund-raising and enables leaders to attract and motivate staff and volunteers. Even when they possess them, nonprofit leaders are seldom recognized or rewarded for their managerial qualities, and they are often pulled toward other priorities.

This situation is beginning to change. Many nonprofit organizations are investing to train and develop their management teams, including next-generation leaders. Schools of business and policy are devoting more resources to the management and leadership of nonprofits, thereby providing an expanding cohort of young people eager to enter the social sector. Nonprofit boards and executive directors are also becoming increasingly willing to consider hiring "bridgers." These are men and women who want to bring the skills and management experience they've developed in their business careers to social-sector organizations (though not surprisingly, compensation can still be the sticking point in such hires).

Funders, too, are paying more attention to what it takes to develop and maintain great nonprofit leadership. The Social Enterprise Initiative started at Harvard Business School by John Whitehead and an innovative sabbatical program created by the Los Angeles–based Durfee Foundation offer two examples.

When John Whitehead, former cochair of Goldman Sachs and a deputy secretary of state during the Reagan administration, returned to New York from Washington, DC, in 1989, he made a surprising decision: to work with nonprofits, rather than return to the business world. "I wanted to participate, not just by giving to these organizations, but by helping manage and run them, and by working for them as they did their good work," he recalls.[6]

Unsurprisingly, Whitehead's expertise was in high demand. "One thing led to another, and suddenly I was chairing ten different nonprofit boards!" Recognizing that he could not contribute sufficiently to so many organizations, Whitehead soon scaled back his involvement. But his cross-organizational perspective left him troubled by what he perceived as a lack of individuals with managerial skills, not only at the senior level, but also among the young people entering nonprofits.

Seeking a way to build capacity for the entire sector, he approached the dean of Harvard Business School, John McArthur, in the early 1990s to see if the school would consider teaching courses in nonprofit management. With such a program, Whitehead thought, a new pool of talent, trained in management, would be prepared to enter nonprofits and ultimately take on leadership positions.

McArthur was enthusiastic, and Whitehead agreed to invest $500,000 a year for three years running to see if the idea could get off the ground. The planning proved successful, and in 1993 Whitehead funded the creation of a permanent Social Enterprise Initiative.

Over the next ten years, the initiative grew to seven full-time faculty members, with three dozen more making part-time commitments to the field. The group has written dozens of teaching cases, introduced six new courses into the second-year curriculum, hosted major conferences, and produced numerous working papers, award-winning books, and articles. Students not only flock to the new social enterprise courses, but also devote scarce free time to working with nonprofit organizations. The student-run Social Enterprise Club, which was essentially moribund in the early 1990s, had 320 members by 2003 and is now one of the largest and most active clubs on the campus.

Following the launch of the Social Enterprise Initiative, many other business schools introduced nonprofit programs of their own. "This is just what I hoped, but couldn't expect, would happen," Whitehead observes. "Everyone has some program now. Good nonprofit management is considered to be absolutely essential."

The Durfee Foundation created its hallmark sabbatical program in response to a parallel challenge, keeping strong nonprofit leaders inspired and energized. With assets of just under $25 million, the foundation supports arts and culture, education, and community development in the LA region. The sabbatical program was born when foundation staff noticed a disturbing trend. "Executive directors were leaving their jobs, even though they liked them and were good at them. But they couldn't see any other way to take a break," Durfee president Caroline Avery explains. "They were approaching, or past, burnout."[7]

Eager to help, Durfee designed the program, which gives six nonprofit leaders a year stipends of up to $35,000 to take a minimum of three months off. Based on suggestions from the leaders themselves, Durfee made the program totally flexible; the recipients can choose to spend the time however they wish.[8] "Only they can know what will best rejuvenate them," Avery says, "so why would we try to tell them what to do?"

Durfee has seen remarkable results from paying leaders not to work. In a study of several sabbatical programs, including Durfee's, three-quarters of the participants reported that the time away helped them develop their organization's vision, or frame a new one.[9] Awardees also said they returned feeling more confident in their ability to take on challenges and grapple with problems.

Perhaps most significant, the sabbatical program also helped their organizations grow new leaders. A full 83 percent of the awardees believe their managers became more skillful, thanks to the opportunity to step up and develop new capabilities in their interim positions. Some 60 percent also noted that their boards had become more effective as a result of the preparation for and learning that accompanied the sabbatical.[10] Durfee and other foundations with similar programs, like Boston's Barr Foundation, are addressing the nonprofit sector's leadership shortage effectively and creatively.

Efforts like these notwithstanding, nonprofits continue to face significant leadership and management challenges because of the way they are customarily funded. Bridgespan colleagues have studied the sector's funding issues at length; one of their key observations concerns the prevalence of what they call the "nonprofit starvation cycle."[11]

The nonprofit starvation cycle. The cycle begins with funders (public as well as private) who have unrealistically low assumptions about what it actually costs to run a nonprofit. Nonprofits, dependent on the public for funding, feel obliged to conform to those unrealistic expectations insofar as humanly possible. To that end, they cut their overhead to the bone (a choice often reinforced by their desire to "spend every nickel on the kids") and underreport their expenditures in annual reports, IRS 990s, and fundraising materials, to make their operations look as "lean" as possible. This, in turn, only reinforces the unrealistically low assumptions that kicked off the cycle in the first place. And so the cycle repeats itself. Over time, funders expect grantees to do more and more with less and less.

These leadership and funding challenges intersect in troubling ways. Nonprofit leaders are typically under relentless pressure to raise money to support existing programs and, if they are truly fortunate, to innovate, improve, and do more. As a result, they're perpetually in "sell mode," externally focused and intent on persuading people to contribute their money, time, and influence. Even the most successful nonprofits usually have to raise the funds for each year's operating budget anew. Their leaders never forget that if they come up short in that effort, the organization's very existence may be imperiled.

This reality is one that many funders with business backgrounds simply cannot comprehend. How, they wonder, can a seemingly successful organization not have the necessary financial sophistication to manage its cash flow or put money aside for the inevitable rainy day. The answer lies in the starvation cycle described above, and the relentless pressure to cut overhead. A CFO is overhead, pure and simple. But to underscore the distinction we made earlier, it would be hard to argue that, for most nonprofits, a capable CFO would be "bad" overhead. While it's wrong to waste philanthropic dollars on goods and services that aren't needed, it's equally wrong to limit the impact of philanthropic dollars by depriving nonprofits of the funds they need to sustain, improve, and expand their performance ("good" overhead).

What, exactly, is good overhead? Experienced managers can answer this question easily (although, of course, the specifics vary from setting to setting). Good overhead is a human resource system that helps to develop people and build an organization's managerial bench strength. Good overhead is a functional information technology setup that helps the organization track its results, learn what's working, and commit more resources in productive directions. Good overhead is a chief operating officer who can take on the responsibility for managing the organization's administrative systems, leaving the executive director free to focus on program issues and developing funding.

Here, too, there are signs of change. A number of leading foundations, such as the Edna McConnell Clark Foundation, the Packard Foundation, and the Hewlett Foundation, have committed sizable sums of money to building their grantees' organizational capacity, as a means to their achieving more and better results. Nonprofits, too, are changing. Their leaders are increasingly willing to allocate resources to acquiring, developing, and retaining skilled managers. They are thinking strategically about their funding model (rather than simply running from one financial emergency to the next). Their boards are engaged, and bringing their own talents and networks to bear to make their organizations more effective and efficient.

These are positive trends that are likely to continue, and which you can help perpetuate through your own philanthropy. What do you need to do? First, be aware of these pernicious capacity issues, and don't underestimate the extent to which they can undermine the results you seek. Second, work to build a true partnership with your grantees, so that they and you can address these issues and see better results. This is the subject to which we turn next.

5

HOW DO I WORK
WITH GRANTEES?

ONORS AND FOUNDATION GRANT MAKERS
often talk about "partnering" with their grantees.
The description is well intended, but it's seldom
the felt reality for the nonprofit leaders with whom they are
working. The latter certainly appreciate the dollars their
benefactors are providing. But the relationship? Let's just say
that "partnership" isn't usually the first word that comes to
mind.

Does this matter? Yes, because the ability to work effectively with your grantees is the fundamental operating requirement in the journey from aspirations to real impact.
They, not you, are on the ground, doing most (if not all) of
the heaviest lifting. So it's really not much of a stretch to say
that your single most important job is choosing your grantees
wisely, then doing everything you can to help them deliver
the best possible results.

For the most part, developing an effective relationship with
your grantees, one that each of you might honestly characterize as a partnership, is not all that different from developing

any other healthy human relationship. It starts with some sort of common interest. It requires a willingness to understand the other person's point of view, to make the effort to see the world through his or her eyes. It is reinforced or undermined by the quality of your interactions, day by day, and year by year.

What is different about philanthropic relationships is that, because of the enormous power imbalance between those who have money and those who need it, the donor always has the upper hand. The fact that you control the resources on which the grantee organization's work depends is never far from the nonprofit leader's mind. This reality inevitably tempers his or her willingness to be candid, and to provide vital feedback—about what's working and what's not, or about the impact of a donor's requests on the organization's ability to perform. The problem is that you need such information almost as much as the grantee does, in order to avoid becoming complacent and falling into the trap of satisfactory underperformance.

How can you avoid this problematic outcome? Effective donor-grantee relationships come in many shapes and sizes, but they usually have two distinctive hallmarks. One is that the donor and the grantee have reached and maintain a shared definition of success: their goals are truly strategically aligned. The other is that their working relationship is productive, by which we mean that both partners benefit, because the relationship enhances the grantee's ability to generate results.

When donor-grantee relationships go awry, the real victims are neither the donors nor their grantees, but the communities and people they aspire to help and the problems they seek to solve. The aim of this chapter, therefore, is to help both philanthropists and their grantees understand what it takes to build and sustain real-world partnerships, so they can work together more effectively on society's behalf. In that spirit, we'll start with an example of a truly extraordinary partnership that is transforming the lives of thousands of young people throughout the United States.

EDNA MCCONNELL CLARK FOUNDATION: PARTNERING FOR YOUNG PEOPLE

The Edna McConnell Clark Foundation (EMCF), which you've encountered in earlier chapters, supports organizations that help low-income youth, ages nine through twenty-four, achieve positive outcomes related to their education, employment, and avoidance of risky behavior. But given its theory of change, which focuses on helping high-performing organizations build the capacity they need to deliver ever better results to growing numbers of youth, EMCF looks for more than an alignment around mission when selecting grantees. As president Nancy Roob explains, "We look for organizations that are really expert in making a difference around this issue. Once we've found them, we invest in their ability to produce more results, and to get more impact."[1]

With investments that span multiple years and multiple millions of dollars, EMCF has a high stake in forming genuine partnerships with its grantees. These partnerships begin with finding the right grantees, a process to which the foundation devotes considerable resources. Staff and independent experts scan and scour the youth development field to find organizations already achieving impressive results. In some cases, these organizations don't even know the foundation exists. Youth Villages was one such organization.

Youth Villages, the Tennessee-based nonprofit dedicated to helping emotionally and behaviorally troubled children and their families through counseling, residential services, and other interventions, has long benefitted from the support of individual philanthropists like Clarence Day, described in chapter 2. Its relationship with EMCF began when CEO Patrick Lawler received a phone call out of the blue, saying that the foundation would be interested in learning more about them. "They literally got a call saying, 'We've been doing research, and you've popped up on our radar,'" Roob recalls. "And I think they were pretty psyched to get the call, because they had little exposure to national foundations. This is usually a pretty happy sort of phone call to get from somebody."

After several conversations, it was clear that the foundation and Youth Villages were aligned around their mutual dedication to getting more and better results for youth. So Clark kicked off its rigorous "due diligence" process to get to know the organization. In addition to multiple site visits and leadership meetings, Lawler and his team had to provide countless documents and data, yet he remembers the process not as a burden, but as a pleasant surprise. "This process helped us know they were serious about wanting to see how our programs work. They weren't just coming in for a quick visit. They met with us, our local funders, and most of our board. And they understood our field and, therefore, our outcomes. We don't get a lot of people with a lot of resources really asking about the work, but Clark did that."[2]

After these visits and research, the foundation offered Youth Villages a grant to undertake business planning. As Roob sees it, business planning is both a critical piece of the selection process and the first step in building a relationship with a prospective grantee. "Business planning is a very important beginning to the relationship, because lots of stuff comes up. Hard decisions have to get made, trade-offs and strategic choices. And we are at the table during many of those key discussions. It's during this phase that we set the right tone for the relationship, which is about supporting the leadership and the board to make the decisions they want to make. Our role in the process is to hold up the mirror and try to add value by asking the right questions."

Lawler also recalls this process as key for Youth Villages. "We had our mission and values to direct where we were going. But this process helped us really focus in on where we felt we could provide the greatest impact and have the best outcomes. And it was great to have Clark there because they understood everything so quickly, in terms of our service to the field."

Jointly committed to the plan that emerged, Clark agreed to a multiyear investment in Youth Villages that set performance milestones rather than restrictions on how the funds were to be used. "When we find the right organization, they're the experts, we're not," Roob points out. "They want to be able to do more. They want to be able to meet their aspirations. That's where we help."

Coupling respect for Youth Villages' expertise, strategy, and ability to execute with dedication to providing what the organization really needed, Clark has worked with Youth Villages for six years, providing grants and also including the organization in its innovative Growth Capital Aggregation Pilot. Throughout this time, each has been realistic about what to expect from the other. "We're both committed to this plan," says Roob, "but stuff happens, and they won't meet every milestone, and they will need to change course. And our expectation is that we're not expecting 100 percent performance, but we are expecting no surprises."

From Lawler's perspective, the foundation's contributions are unique in several ways, including its ability to draw on its deep knowledge of all its grantees. "They have the ability to compare across groups," he reflects. "They know what can work and what usually doesn't—in leadership, finance, outcomes, information technology, the works."

Since 2004, Clark has invested more than $20 million in Youth Villages to help it implement its business plan. During this time, Youth Villages has begun working in four new states and Washington, DC, and has almost tripled the number of young people it serves annually. As of 2010, Youth Villages was providing more than eighteen thousand children with benefits for them and their families that persist for years. Data collected in 2010 indicate that a full two years after discharge, 81 percent of the children they served were still at home or in a homelike environment, and 85 percent were in school, had graduated, or were enrolled in GED classes.[3]

CHOOSING WELL:
FACTS OVER INFATUATION

The "who first" principle applies at least as forcefully to selecting your grantees as it does to your own philanthropy.

Get this decision right on the front end, and you can minimize (or even head off entirely) a lot of other problems downstream. Get this decision wrong, and there's not much you can do later on to recover. As Nancy Roob points out, "The most important thing we do is selection. And if we don't select well everything is downhill from that point forward."

Although it may feel counterintuitive, zeroing in on the right grantees begins with increasing the "deal flow" by expanding the pool of candidates you consider. To be confident that the organizations you choose are the best for the job, you first need to understand the universe of nonprofits that might be contenders. Restricting your search to the handful of nonprofits you already know means you may unwittingly miss the chance of achieving significantly better results. Finding new organizations can be laborious, especially if you are working on your own, or have only a small staff to rely on. Nevertheless, this important step, known as "sourcing," is worth the effort.

How might you begin? Four Rs—relationships, research, respected opinions, and requests—provide good ways to start, although you should certainly complement them with innovative ideas of your own. First, explore the *relationships* you already have, but be creative: ask knowledgeable colleagues, independent experts, or other philanthropists to highlight promising organizations in your field of interest. One director of a family foundation (she is also its sole staff member) routinely seeks suggestions from peers at larger foundations active in its area of giving. Although the nonprofits they recommend may not have been good fits for the larger institutions, they are often ideal candidates for investment from her smaller, more focused foundation.

Research can also bring new names to your attention. A philanthropist we know who is still fully engaged in his business career finds many of his most successful grantees by reading the newspaper, and following up on the stories that captivate him. A more rigorous version of this approach would be to do a formal "landscape analysis," which involves mapping all the major and minor players in your field of interest. At the national level, this can be very resource intensive. But if you're engaged at a community or regional level, it can be a helpful and manageable exercise, even if you're an individual acting on your own. A conversation with your local community foundation leadership, for example, will often yield reliable information about nearby organizations doing good work in your area of interest.

Seeking *respected opinions* from experts can also yield new and promising names to consider. Peter and Carolyn Lynch rely on their board of directors, all experts in their particular fields, to suggest new organizations that might merit support. Because the board members have a deep understanding of the foundation's mission and values to complement their expertise, their suggestions often lead to high-potential grantee opportunities.

Finally, depending on your scope and presence in the field, issuing *requests* for new grantees may bring excellent and hitherto unknown nonprofits to your attention. Since most philanthropists are already inundated with funding requests, this can be a mixed blessing. But if you use your strategy to establish and publicize the specific criteria you are seeking, you may find that the quality of the responses is surprisingly high. This approach requires the capacity to do some significant outreach, however, as well as to review what will likely be a large number of applicants. So if you're drawn to this approach, you have to be mindful of the resources you will need to do the job well, in a timely manner. Soliciting requests, and then leaving respondents hanging for months on end, will not only make it hard to get off to a productive start with the grantees you ultimately select, but also compromise your reputation with others in the field.

GIVE DILIGENCE ITS DUE

Once you're confident that you have a strong pool of potential grantees, significant work lies ahead. Specifically, before you decide where to commit, you need to kick the tires; that is, perform the philanthropic equivalent of "due diligence." The purpose of this screening process is to develop an informed point of view about a prospect's capacity to deliver results (both from the program side and in terms of its organizational capacity), and about the kinds of support they need (from you and others) to do that.

Due diligence can be tricky, because as soon as you contact a nonprofit for information, you'll raise expectations. And the more information you ask for, the higher those expectations will become (regardless of what you say), and the more work it will cause the nonprofit. So it is always wise to do as much secondary work as possible before reaching out, and to be as clear as possible when you do connect about what you're looking for and what your process and timeline will be.

The magnitude of the grant you're considering and the context in which you're working will largely determine how rigorous your due diligence needs to be. A potential grant may be a relatively small component of a complex initiative, or a major, sustaining, stand-alone investment; a "big bet" with a multiple-year timeline, or a small, one-time, special-purpose gift. It may require tight coordination with other donors and nonprofits, or stand entirely on its own. Similarly, all the important links in your strategy may be proven, or it may contain a number of important unknowns.

Your line of sight as the decision maker is also relevant. You (and others involved in your philanthropy) may have little previous knowledge of a potential grantee, or you may be actively involved as one of its volunteers or board members. If you are a foundation executive, you may have unilateral decision-making authority, or be part of a complex internal decision-making process involving multiple players, detailed documentation, and exacting processes. In short, the form and intensity of the due diligence process should be keyed to the circumstances, with your goal being to avoid "avoidable mistakes," the ones you could easily have seen coming had you only taken the time to look.

John Morgridge, former head of Cisco Systems and chair of the board of The Nature Conservancy (TNC), and Nancy Roob and her colleagues at the Edna McConnell Clark Foundation (EMCF) offer two ends of the due diligence spectrum. Having served on TNC's board beginning in 1998, Morgridge is intimately familiar with the organization, its leadership and its strategic direction. As a result, John and his wife, Tashia, have been able to make significant contributions totaling multiple millions of dollars with confidence, knowing that he has been effectively engaged in due diligence for over a decade.

Conversely, donors considering deep investments and exploring new nonprofits require a more formal and rigorous due diligence process. EMCF, for example, evaluates prospective grantees, like Youth Villages, on twenty-one separate indicators and performs multiday site visits with an organization's leadership before making an initial, relatively small grant. Then the new grantee typically engages in a business-planning process, funded by the initial grant, before the foundation makes its go or no-go decision about additional funding. Because EMCF is committing to both a multimillion-dollar investment and a multiyear relationship when it fully takes on a new grantee, this complex and lengthy due diligence process is not only appropriate but essential.

Due diligence doesn't have to be elaborate to be sufficient. Some results-focused philanthropists with few, if any, staff routinely engage in multiple in-depth conversations with a prospective grantee's leadership (including selected board members) about their vision and aims. Others narrow in on a short list of criteria. San Francisco–based Tipping Point Community, for example, looks at just four program requirements—such as whether the organization serves low-income clients, Tipping Point's target beneficiaries, and will commit to tracking outcomes—and three organizational requirements, including financial health and willingness to work with a deeply engaged funder. The criteria are not elaborate, but they help Tipping Point's decision makers assess whether a prospective grantee is aligned with its strategy and capable of producing results.[4]

As this discussion demonstrates, the degree of rigor your selection process demands will always be case specific. Still, there are several clear and compelling rules of thumb that apply pretty much universally.

You will get what you pay for. Skimping on due diligence, whether because of personal infatuation, a flawed process, or an inadequate investment of time and effort, will almost certainly come back to haunt you. Mistakes can be expensive and difficult to remedy; once a commitment is made, it can be hard to unwind. Even if you decide that you want to change course with a grantee, it will likely prove difficult, and be potentially damaging to them and to you.

Recognizing this sobering fact, some philanthropists go too far in the opposite direction. Perhaps because they lack confidence in their judgment, or because they fear making a mistake that might become visible and embarrassing, they pull back from significant commitments. They dabble, instead of making grants big enough to do some real good. Putting a toe in the water may be fine if that's a way of testing the waters before making a larger commitment. All too often, though, a habit of superficial investigation leads to a portfolio of overly modest grants that go nowhere. When you are truly interested in a prospective grantee, investing the time to dig deeper, and building the confidence to make a substantial grant, will often translate to better results.

Effective due diligence is a process of mutual discovery. Certainly, this includes assembling cold hard facts about a potential grantee's programs and finances. But it should go beyond that, to issues like compatibility and the prospects for developing a mutually committed and trusting relationship. Diligence is the first step in building a productive working relationship with your grantees. Underinvesting undermines selection, but it can also undermine the potential for a strong relationship going forward.

Yes, this takes time. If you feel that you don't have that kind of time, or if you simply want to begin learning about a new realm and benefit from others' experience as you start down the path, you might consider piggybacking on another philanthropist's effort, as the investors in the GreenLight Fund do. (Of course, you will still need to do some due diligence on the other philanthropist or intermediary.) Warren Buffett's $31 billion gift to the Bill & Melinda Gates Foundation stands as the biggest philanthropic piggyback in history—and a model for leveraging the experience of other donors. This isn't taking the easy way out but, rather, the opposite. The choice you have to invest in other donors' work is an extraordinary opportunity that may help to generate near-term results that you couldn't otherwise come close to achieving.

You need to be disciplined. It is human nature to fall in love with a deal. You may get swept up in the cause of the moment. (Philanthropy is just as subject to fads and the "new new thing" as any other sphere.) Or you may be impressed by, and personally fond of, the individual leading a particular initiative. While we'd never advise ignoring your instincts, it's also wise to remember that charisma probably played a significant part in his or her rise to prominence. As one philanthropist ruefully pointed out, "Plenty of people have interesting ideas, but at the end of the day they don't have the leadership or management skills to drive an organization forward. That's a very, very rare skill set. As a philanthropist, I may get enamored of an idea, but then, over time, I realize that the leader is just not implementing."[5] So when confronted with an exciting leader, be inspired, but also be disciplined about whether he or she has the skills to drive results.

As for the cause of the moment, keep in mind the near total absence of marketplace dynamics and indicators that we described in earlier chapters. New ideas appear constantly, but there are very few forces working to weed out the less promising ones. At the same time, there is a widespread and persistent bias in philanthropy toward new programs and organizations. While measured and intentional support of innovation and discovery is critical, uncritical fascination with the next big thing can vacuum up funding that might have been better directed toward high-performing nonprofits already doing excellent work.

The story of one would-be generous couple shows the consequences—for them, for other donors, and for the institution they wanted to support—of neglecting to engage in appropriate due diligence. Mary and Tom Miller, as we'll call them here, committed $10 million as the anchor gift for the silent phase of their local science museum's capital campaign. They were passionate about science, and the charismatic director pitched a compelling vision: besides funding a spectacular new wing, their gift would enable the museum to become the centerpiece of the city they loved. The museum also found donors to match the Millers' gift, dollar for dollar.

Things blew up just as the museum was about to launch the public phase of the campaign. Tom had finally reviewed the expansion plans, and quickly discovered serious flaws in the financial assumptions on which it was based. Adjusted to reflect reality, the plan would have the museum bleeding red ink. Tom and Mary confronted the director, who defended the plan. Eventually they withdrew their pledge, causing most of the matching funds to disappear as well.

The museum cancelled the project and replaced it with a modest remodeling. Local media picked up on the story with a spin that suggested the museum had been negligent. Previously loyal donors withdrew their annual support. The executive director was ultimately fired. Years later, the institution is still not back on track.

While this is a story in which all sides share the blame, it amply illustrates the value of due diligence. Had the Millers been more rigorous in examining the proposal, they might not have signed on, or they might have been able to help the museum shape a more realistic strategy, thereby averting catastrophe. The moral: don't let opinion—or infatuation—override facts. The two matter equally.

You need to be realistic. In light of the sectorwide capacity issues we discussed in the previous chapter, you shouldn't be surprised if your due diligence process uncovers some serious organizational deficiencies in an otherwise highly promising prospective grantee. The salient question, then, is whether these deficiencies can be successfully remedied. The answer will depend as much on whether the organization is able to undertake capacity building (and the inevitable accompanying organizational changes) as on your willingness to consider funding some or all of the nonprogram expenses that would involve.

If a nonprofit's leaders and board are unable or unwilling to tackle (or even acknowledge) their organizational issues, there's not very much that you or anyone else can do about it. (There's little point in providing the funding to design and implement a performance management system, for instance, if the executive director considers annual reviews "administrivia.") But as the Edna McConnell Clark Foundation's experience demonstrates, the converse is equally true. When the will to build the capacity to deliver better results exists among an organization's leadership, helping them develop the people, processes, and financial model required to do that can be enormously leveraged, and generate huge impact.

Realism is equally essential with respect to a prospective grantee's strategy. Just as a lock will not open unless the tumblers line up, unlocking social impact requires strategic alignment between you and your grantees. How you can achieve such alignment and what gets in the way are the topics we'll consider next.

A SHARED DEFINITION OF SUCCESS

Achieving genuine alignment requires clarity on both sides of the donor-grantee equation about what is strategically in, and out, of bounds. That is why the time you invest beforehand to define the results that will constitute success for your philanthropy and your strategy for achieving them are so important. The same is true for your grantees. Just as you have to be clear about your goals and role, the nonprofit leaders with whom you work have to be equally clear about the results they hold themselves accountable for, and how their organization will deliver them. Absent shared strategic clarity, grounded in facts, both of you are likely to fall short.

Using your goals as the lens, there are basically two ways to approach aligning with a grantee. One is to identify organizations (or individuals) whose goals are compatible with your own, then support their work in its entirety. The other is to align with a grantee around one or more of its programs or initiatives (existing or to be created). The Edna McConnell Clark Foundation's multimillion-dollar grants to select youth-serving nonprofits primed to expand offer one example of the first approach. The work of the John M. Olin Foundation provides another.

John Olin was an American businessman whose wealth derived from chemical and munitions manufacturing. In the 1950s and 1960s, Olin became more and more concerned about the strength of the free-market system, which he deeply valued and trusted. He knew that public policy could help protect free markets, and he saw law and philosophy as important levers to influence such policy.

With this in mind, Olin directed the John M. Olin Foundation to "provide support for projects that reflect or are intended to strengthen the economic, political and cultural institutions upon which the American heritage of constitutional government and private enterprise is based."[6] To this end, the foundation supported legal associations, like the Federalist Society, conservative scholars, and a variety of conservative think tanks focused on scholarly and legal advocacy, like the Heritage Foundation and the Manhattan Institute.

In its selection process, the foundation chose organizations and researchers that shared Olin's philosophy. Confident that their grantees' work would align with John Olin's wishes, the foundation's leaders felt no need to micromanage the funds. (To prevent his wealth from being misspent through "mission drift," Olin also required that all the foundation's assets be spent within a generation of his death.) The foundation distributed some $370 million over several decades, a relatively small amount (compared, for instance, to the Ford Foundation, which gave away nearly $500 million in 2009 alone).[7] Yet many believe that the John M. Olin Foundation did more, through its strategic giving, to institutionalize and sustain the conservative movement than any other group in the last generation.[8]

The second and more common way in which donors and grantees align strategically is at the program or initiative level. Sometimes a single program or set of programs is attractive because it fills a specific link in a donor's theory of change. The Gordon and Betty Moore Foundation's grant to a marine research organization falls into this category.

The Moore Foundation seeks "to improve the quality of life for future generations."[9] Part of that broad mandate includes environmental conservation and, in that context, connecting conservation and human well being. Through its Marine Conservation Initiative, launched in 2005, Moore has committed approximately $145 million, over ten years, to help create resilient and productive marine ecosystems in the United States and Canada through various means, including reforming fisheries management.

Fisheries management is a topic that concerns a wide range of stakeholders, including federal, state, and local governments, environmentalists, and fishermen and fish processing plant operators. The Moore Foundation has involved itself in this complex field through a series of strategic grants that focus on a variety of approaches to reforming existing management practices (such as scientifically based catch limits and better monitoring) and include stakeholders in the new system's design.

In 2007, the foundation made a $1.1 million grant to the Gulf of Maine Research Institute (GRMI), a Portland, Maine–based marine science center with strong links to the community and a reputation as a neutral party in fisheries management. While GMRI engages in many kinds of research and educational activities,[10] Moore's 2007 grant focused on communications and convening, as well as providing, technical expertise to enable stakeholders to develop, and therefore support, a sustainable fisheries management program in New England.[11]

In other cases, an organization will be an attractive candidate for programmatic funding because it is particularly well equipped to take on a new initiative with your backing. The Lynch Leadership Academy at Boston College is one such example. Peter and Carolyn Lynch share a passion for education that is rooted in their personal knowledge of the lifelong impact good schooling can have. In 2010, the Lynch Foundation, which supports a number of Boston-area and national educational institutions and programs, announced the creation of a new "educational leadership academy" at Boston College's Lynch School of Education. With an initial endowment of $20 million, the academy will be the first in the nation to jointly train and support principals from Catholic, public, and charter schools.[12]

Carolyn Lynch describes the impetus for the new academy this way. "Ask teachers what they need, and they'll tell you that they need better principals. Ask principals what *they* need, and they'll say that they need more training. That's what this new academy, and the principals' certificate program it will offer, are all about."[13] While Boston College obviously pursues a huge number of worthy educational initiatives, the Lynches focused on the one that aligned the need they, and the education sector, saw as most important.

The power of strategic alignment is its ability to create value for society by combining forces for good. It is so transparently productive that it should be standard operating procedure for every philanthropist and nonprofit leader. If only that were true!

STRATEGIC DISRUPTION

Philanthropy is a buyers' market, and nonprofit leaders are seldom in a position to negotiate aggressively with potential donors. On the contrary, the selection process is (and feels) quite one sided, as though potential grantees are participating in a beauty contest in which the only imperative is to please the judges. So, for better or worse, the views of an individual donor (especially a very large one) can strongly influence grantee behavior. Often this influence will take the form of tweaks to an existing program, or the addition of a new activity, more or less aligned with the nonprofit's existing strategy, about which a leading donor is enthusiastic. When such an intervention is supported on the donor's part by deep knowledge of the field, it can provide helpful input to the grantee's strategy.

But when an ambitious donor forces a strategy on a basically unwilling grantee and the grantee, lured by the money, rolls over, the ensuing strategic disruption can be quite costly. It can distort an otherwise cogent strategy. It can add excess expense and irritate (or alienate) other donors and stakeholders. In the end, it can shortchange society by undermining the organization's overall capacity to perform.

Just this sort of strategic disruption occurred when a midwestern foundation approached an East Coast nonprofit that was becoming known for providing job-training services to welfare mothers. Excited by preliminary data, which indicated that the program was showing success in mitigating this intractable problem, a senior program officer proposed funding a second site near the foundation's headquarters. Tempted by the prospective donor's generosity, flattered to be courted, and under constant pressure to grow, the nonprofit's leader couldn't refuse the invitation to expand, even though the organization's top priority was still refining its program model and strengthening its existing operation.

As is often the case, while early results showed that the program was working, participants received a wide range of services, and it was unclear which of those services actually mattered most in terms of yielding results. At the same time, the organization hadn't yet grappled with a number of hard questions required for effective replication. For example, they weren't sure which contextual factors were essential to the program's success. At the original site, they had a strong base in the community and an alliance with local government officials. Would both those factors be necessary elsewhere? The organization had planned to devote time and resources to questions like this, but the temptation of immediate funding to open in a new city with thousands of deserving welfare moms to serve was irresistible.

Unsurprisingly, the new site was a disappointment. The foundation could not afford to fund the full program, and the organization hadn't built relationships with any other local funders to fill the gap. Short on funds, the nonprofit chose to provide a scaled back suite of services, but the new combination failed to produce the original outcomes. Meanwhile, the original site hit a plateau while attention was diverted elsewhere. Several years later, the organization had a failing operation and a program model still in need of refinement. Good intentions, minus strategic alignment, simply derailed both organizations and wasted resources neither could afford to squander.

Could this train wreck have been averted? Probably. But not without a different set of conversations and some different behavior on both sides of the table. The foundation's program officer would have had to be willing to begin the interaction by respecting the nonprofit leader's experiences, and fully understanding his views. The latter would have had to be both disciplined and candid about communicating his organization's strategy, and what its real needs were. Had such conversations occurred, the upshot might well have been a decision not to go forward. Disappointing as that might have been in the short term, it would have been a far better outcome than what actually ensued.

Why don't conversations like the one hypothesized above happen more often? The root of the problem is the inherent power imbalance between donors and grantees, and the way it drives up the real cost of philanthropic capital for nonprofit grantees.

THE COST OF PHILANTHROPIC CAPITAL

Just as businesses incur a cost of capital, nonprofit organizations pay a price for the money they raise. The true costs of their fund-raising are rarely as modest as the direct expenses reported on their public filings, however. More often than not, those figures provide only a baseline on which to add the considerable indirect costs nonprofits incur in the course of raising philanthropic funds: courting prospective funders; preparing and revising grant applications; complying with reporting and monitoring requirements; attending meetings; and all the other activities that are part and parcel of "doing business" with philanthropists and foundations. Although these costs are very real, they are almost never quantified, because time (especially senior management time), not money, is the coin in which most of them are paid.

The problem isn't the fact that there is a cost of capital. Philanthropic resources (nonfinancial as well as financial) provide significant benefits, and no sensible nonprofit leader would expect those benefits to come cost free. The problem is that, all too often, the cost of capital escalates out of control, because a grantee's chronic need for funding motivates its leadership to accept whatever terms and conditions a major contributor imposes, even if that results in management disruptions, organizational constraints, or strategic distractions. Meanwhile, the donors, for their part, have little incentive to try to mitigate the costs or modify their behavior, because the burdens they are imposing remain essentially invisible and free, at least for them.

One well-regarded nonprofit leader recounted a particularly harrowing story that illustrates the kind of burdens philanthropists routinely—and unwittingly—impose, which drive up the cost of capital.

A billionaire passed away, leaving his fortune to be administered by three longtime employees. The employees, who were not wealthy and had no experience with philanthropy, suddenly found themselves required to distribute upward of $30 million a year entirely on their own.

Our friend led a large national network that provides after-school programs for inner-city schools. He and his development team heard about the new foundation and sought a meeting with its novice philanthropists. The latter were receptive and enthusiastic, and the two groups quickly entered an extended "getting to know you" period. The funders met with some of the national network's board members, went on site visits, and indicated serious interest in helping grow the organization's national footprint. Encouraged by their enthusiasm, the network submitted a request for $10 million to support expansion to four new cities over four years.

After a two-month wait, the funders finally replied that they weren't interested in a major gift after all, but would like to make a smaller commitment. They would consider supporting a couple of schools in full, covering everything necessary to achieve good results. Could the executive director pull together a proposal like that?

Setting aside their disappointment (and frustration), the executive director, his development team, and some of the local offices put together a thorough and compelling proposal that fit the new description. They researched the best sites and carefully calculated the costs, which included transportation for the students and national office staff to support the start-up as well as staff on site in the new locations. The price tag came to just under $1 million over three years.

More long weeks went by without a word from the funders. Finally, they replied that the numbers didn't seem quite right. According to their calculations, "overhead" accounted for 40 percent of the proposal's cost, and they were unwilling to consider anything over 15 percent. "Direct program costs," like the new staff, were fine; funding for the national staff or transportation was not. The executive director was astonished. Without transportation, the kids couldn't get to the programs. And without support from the national staff, the new sites would be reinventing the wheel, without any of the deep expertise the network had already developed.

Unable to agree, the funders and the nonprofit soon parted ways. For the funders, it was just another rejection. For the nonprofit, it was nine months of senior staff time and hundreds of hours of work thrown away.

In addition to wasting precious time and imposing unrealistic demands, grant makers (donors, trustees, and foundation staff alike) can easily fall into the trap of behaving like owners with formal control, instead of financial intermediaries with an ability to exercise influence. As an illustration, consider what happened a few years back at a wealthy new foundation, which recruited a cadre of very bright people, all new to the fields in which the donor wanted to engage.

In the course of the first year, the foundation's senior staff designed a "breakthrough" strategy and identified potential grantees who they thought might be able to execute on the foundation's ambitious goals. In effect, prospective grantees were asked to explain what they could do to serve the foundation's needs, with little consideration given to their own extensive experience or existing strategic plans. The nonprofits went along, writing compelling proposals, even when they knew that the initiatives would conflict with their own strategic priorities. The unstated message from the foundation was clear and clearly received: "If you want our money, you had best do things our way."

Before long, it became equally clear that the foundation's executives *were not* more knowledgeable than their grantees. The foundation's strategy was both untested and confused. Worst of all, by insisting that grantees blindly conform to its needs, rather than collaborating, the foundation actually undermined its grantees' performance. This wasn't a partnership of equal players with aligned incentives; it was money throwing its weight around, to the detriment of what the donor had actually set out to achieve.

SEEING THE WORLD
THROUGH YOUR GRANTEE'S EYES

When philanthropists slip into control mode, it also complicates the challenge of bridging the experiential divide that separates them from the nonprofit leaders who receive their funds. While every human relationship has its problems, resolving those problems is considerably easier when each party understands the other's perspective. In the case of philanthropists and grantees, such understanding can be particularly elusive. It's usually less about how much they like one another and more about the realities of the worlds they inhabit, and the worldviews to which their experiences give rise.

Few philanthropists, including those in senior leadership positions in foundations, have ever actually run a nonprofit organization. They may have served on nonprofit boards or acquired deep expertise in a particular field, such as international development or environmental protection. But chances are they haven't spent much of their lives on the front line, working with homeless families, say, or advocating for better maternal health in Africa. Nor have they had to cope with the harsh structural realities that nonprofit leaders routinely confront.

Aside from money, senior management time is a nonprofit organization's most scarce resource. Small leadership teams, limited infrastructure, and modest staff levels can place enormous daily burdens on executive directors and their direct reports, burdens that the most well-intentioned grant makers and donors can unwittingly exacerbate. Proposals are written, and rewritten, then rewritten again, while the decision making stretches out over many months. Funders impose all sorts of measurement requirements, without stopping to ask what's already in place, or whether the measures they're requesting will actually tell them anything useful about the organization's performance. Meetings are convened to share best practices, when what grantees really need are opportunities to meet other high-net-worth philanthropists who might be interested in funding their kind of work. Foundation leaders are generous about paying the costs of their grantees' travel, but they never consider the real cost of all those hours, because for them the hours are free.

Diverging worldviews compound the effect of these radically different experiences. For obvious reasons, philanthropists tend to be far more connected to other wealthy and influential individuals than they are to the nonprofit leaders who are their grantees. This self-selection can create a real gap between those dispensing the money and those they rely upon to deliver results. Donors and grantees may appreciate each other's challenges intellectually, and they may even share passions and dreams. But, on a daily basis, they live in dramatically different worlds.

Nothing underscores this more forcefully than the drumbeat of financial urgency, which is basically inaudible to donors but omnipresent for their grantees. Philanthropists seldom lie awake at night, as nonprofit leaders do, worrying about how they will find the funds to make payroll, or maintain a successful program, or purchase laptops that actually work for their staff. If they did, there might be fewer comments like this one, from a well-respected leader of a highly successful nonprofit: "I've been working with this big name donor, modifying one grant renewal request after another for a full ten months. And even after all that, we still have absolutely no idea where we stand."[14]

There are times when philanthropists feel their own special type of agony. During the Great Recession that began in 2008, many foundations suffered major losses in their portfolios. A few downsized, and many cut back on their grant making to preserve capital, often making hard choices in the process about which grantees and commitments to back away from. This was bitter financial medicine, to be sure, but rarely was it an existential threat. (Endowments, even if diminished, were still there, and most staff positions were preserved.) In most cases, the crisis was temporary, and as markets rebounded, commitments were reset to the new realities.

But while donors worry about the allocation of capital, grantees worry about access to it. Even in the best of times, nonprofit organizations typically have few, if any, reserves for critical investments, or for the inevitable rainy day. Some philanthropists even penalize grantees for having rainy-day funds, thinking that "clearly they don't need my money if they have a reserve." And unlike foundations, they cannot bounce back relatively easily when a sagging economy starts to rebound. Given the constant need to pursue prospects and raise funds, it is hardly surprising that a nonprofit leader's most important role is usually "fund-raiser in chief." Or that scrambling for funds to meet the annual budget—so that you can subsequently hit "reset" and start the entire money hunt all over again the next fiscal year—is a fact of life for most executive directors, even in quite well-known and well-supported organizations.

These realities account for the last of the "great divides" that separate donors and grantees: the legitimate but competing incentives that motivate them. Donors want their money to have as much impact as possible, and they want as much assurance as possible that it is being used to absolute best advantage. Grantees share the passion for results and want to get as much money as possible, for as long as possible, with as few limitations on its use as possible.

Ironically, one of the perverse consequences of these competing incentives can be a tacit agreement to avoid hard truths. Grantees see little reason to raise issues or mention shortfalls, lest they compromise the possibility of future funding. And the number of grant makers who really want to hear bad news (that a critical link in the organization's theory of change isn't holding, say) appears fairly small.

Expecting these differences to vanish is unrealistic, but in a healthy relationship they can be minimized and overcome. Choosing grantees with whom you're strategically aligned is the first part of the partnership equation. The second, and more challenging part, is developing a productive working relationship—one that will enable your grantees to achieve better results than they could have done without your help.

DEVELOPING A PRODUCTIVE WORKING RELATIONSHIP

Keeping the cost of capital as reasonable as possible, so that the benefits of working with you outweigh the burdens, is the key to making a donor-grantee relationship truly productive. This, in turn, means being as thoughtful and intentional about how you manage the relationship as you are about making the handful of decisions through which it is chiefly enacted: whom to work with, how to support them, and how, when applicable, to end the relationship in a way that doesn't undermine what you've accomplished together.

Elaine Wynn is the board chair and Dan Cardinali the president of Communities in Schools (CIS). Their relationship provides a good example of the rewards this kind of thoughtfulness and care can return, for the kids they're passionate about helping and for themselves.

Deeply invested in the health of Las Vegas where they built their wealth, Elaine and her former husband, Steve, were especially concerned about the city's high dropout rate. "We had done work with scholarship programs before, but those went to the kids who would be successful no matter what. So we decided to focus on the other end, the kids falling through the cracks," Wynn explains. "I discovered, to my alarm, that many things contributed to putting children at risk of not completing their education. I began desperately, frantically searching for a program to address this for Vegas."[15]

Serendipity stepped in when a friend from Sacramento told her about Bill Milliken, founder of Communities in Schools. "I did research, and invited Bill Milliken to come and meet with us. He described CIS's philosophy and approach in great detail." CIS connects schools with resources that already exist in the community, bringing services, parents, and volunteers into schools to act as a "community of caring adults" to work with educators.[16] "The approach made a tremendous amount of sense to me as a businessperson who understands about leverage," Wynn remembers. "We decided to try a pilot in Las Vegas, and that was the beginning."

In the decades since, Elaine Wynn has expanded her involvement with CIS, where she now serves as chair of the national board. Her commitment to the organization still rests on her belief in, and respect for, the CIS model. For Cardinali this is the most critical part of their relationship: "When we first met, we spent a lot of time talking through the 'DNA level' of the mission. It's a high degree of comfort for me knowing that not only does Elaine understand our mission, she is passionate about it, and she understands the intricacies of the work." According to Cardinali, this same familiarity enables Wynn to contribute more, and more thoughtfully, as a partner in the organization's success: "As I embark on opportunities or leadership challenges, I have someone as a partner and leader whom I can go to and test ideas, without having to explain nuances. How things relate, and why they are challenges, are intuitive to her now."

Wynn and Cardinali have established a partnership that allows room for mistakes, risk-taking, and healthy disagreement. "Elaine encourages testing and exploring ideas, so I don't feel I have to be perfect, and I don't expect her or Bill

[Milliken] to be. We agree that, unless you're pushing boundaries, you'll never maximize results. So, we rarely get in a conflict." Frequent communication, in the form of a standing weekly call, creates a forum for these conversations.

Meanwhile, Elaine has created clear boundaries for her role and been explicit about how and where she can best add value. "I'm not in the trenches, so I try to embrace what happens there, but I leave execution to Dan. My job is keeping us focused on the mission and the vision, and providing guidance on prioritization. Where do we expend energy? What do we grapple with? Very often, my role is to mentor Dan on this. His ideas are never incorrect, but we discuss timing, and when to act on them."

In the ten years that Cardinali and Wynn have worked together, CIS has made exceptional strides. The organization is now reaching 1.3 million students annually, in twenty-five states and Washington, DC.[17] A rigorous national evaluation has shown that CIS both keeps kids in school and increases graduation rates. When the program is implemented faithfully according to the national model, CIS schools have more fourth- and eighth-graders reaching reading and math proficiency than comparison schools.[18]

When nonprofit leaders are asked what, in their experience, distinguishes the best donor-grantee relationships, they invariably cite the same three characteristics: clear communications, consistent expectations, and a sense of mutuality and respect.[19] In essence, they are saying, "Treat us the way you'd want to be treated if our situations were reversed." It sounds simple, but in reality a lot can get in the way, even when there is only one decision maker. When there is more than one, as is usually the case in foundations, the opportunities for confusion and miscommunication increase exponentially.

The fact that grantees have little incentive to tell philanthropists how the relationship is going further complicates communication. The Center for Effective Philanthropy's (CEP) innovative Grantee Perception Report (GPR) provides a powerful way to clear this particular hurdle. CEP administers this survey on a foundation's behalf to all of its grantees, helping it get an accurate—and anonymous—report on what the relationship looks like from the other side. How satisfied are grantees? What can the foundation do better? By providing a safe forum for vital feedback, the GPR has helped more than 190 funders, including such well known foundations as Gates and Packard, improve their relationships with grantees.

Still, even with tools like the GPR, the relationships between grantors and grantees are rarely tidy, even in the most thoughtful and strategic foundations. It's not at all unusual for informal decision-making dynamics to collide with established procedures. This can happen when a benefactor or family member is passionate about a particular program or grant that may not be aligned with the foundation's guidelines. Or communications may get distorted because a program officer pulls back from delivering a tough message, or a potential grantee clings to false hopes by hearing (only) what he or she wants to hear. And creating consistent experiences for grantees is always challenging, not least because attributes like respect and empathy cannot be prescribed.

Moreover, nothing in life is static, and relationships with grantees are no exception to this rule. Even when you have created the platform for a constructive relationship—through careful selection and by "right-sizing" your grant, so it provides the sums of money and kinds of supports a grantee really needs to get the job done—it will require continuing care and vigilance to remain productive. Why? Because the goals you jointly agreed to will likely evolve over time, as the strategy is implemented. And because the relationship itself will ebb and flow, as new information emerges, new needs take shape, and/or new players come into the picture.

Consequently, the more clarity there is on your part, the better—about your strategy and goals; about how and when go/no-go decisions will be made; about the milestones, outputs, and outcomes you expect to see; and about the administrative burdens required to comply with your application and reporting requirements. At the Case Foundation, for example, every commitment has its own grant document, which is short on legalese and long on expectations. "No lawyers work on [these documents]," Jean Case observes. "There are written expectations on both sides around what we're each going to bring to the party, and what we hope to see in return, and what we'll do to evaluate that along the way. We try, with due diligence, to make clear what each side is and is not going to do."[20]

Likewise, when you ask for information, use it. And let your grantee know you're using it. One of the most common sources of frustration for nonprofit leaders is being asked for elaborate reports on their performance and progress which then, as far as they can tell, go absolutely nowhere. As nonprofit leaders frequently lament, "My senior team has spent hundreds of hours preparing detailed material that I doubt anyone ever read. If they did, we certainly didn't hear about it." The irony here is that reviewing and discussing such reports with your grantee can be one of the most constructive aspects of your relationship, as well as one of the most productive.

ENDING HIGH

No donor-grantee relationship is eternal. In discussing his philanthropic work, Brian Olson, the chairman of the board of Civic Builders, a nonprofit whose sole purpose is to develop real estate for charter school operators in New York, underscored the similarities to investment management, especially when it comes to exiting a commitment. "In the investment world," he explains, "you have the constant desire to upgrade your portfolio. That's part of the discipline. And that's true of a well-managed philanthropic portfolio, as well. It sometimes requires breaking with old relationships. But if your goal is to try to obtain the greatest amount of good with the limited resources that you have, it's an inevitable conclusion."[21]

Transitions, whether they involve reducing support or exiting a relationship entirely, are "signature moments" for donors and foundations, and deserve to be managed carefully. First, they signal your values not only to the grantee from whom you're parting, but also to other nonprofits and philanthropists you might want to influence or engage with in the future. And fostering a smooth transition can also allow an about-to-be-former grantee to continue delivering results in an uninterrupted fashion. Finally, as a philanthropist, you have a responsibility to do your best to leave your grantees and those they are serving in a better position than you found them.

By definition, transitions involve decreases in funding, but exactly how this occurs is up to you. Reducing funds gradually, providing matching funds, or adding a few years of additional support on to an expiring grant are all ways to help high-potential grantees bridge the gap while they identify new donors and bring them on board. Help with developing a business plan or funding strategy to address their new circumstances is another possibility, as is using your influence to help solicit new donors, identify new funding sources, or broker a merger or acquisition.

Ensuring a smooth transition is more complicated when the reason you're exiting is that you no longer believe in the organization's strategy and/or its ability to deliver results. In such cases, there is often a fine line between being respectful of your former grantee's reputation (and your own), and stifling honest reflection. Course corrections and failures can teach invaluable lessons, and you'll do everyone a disservice by burying the truth. So navigate carefully, but also remember that what ultimately matters is how this all affects the people or issues you and the organization were jointly aiming to serve.

A PARTNERSHIP, OR A TRAIN WRECK?

One way to conceptualize the donor-grantee relationship is as a matrix, with shared goals and a productive working relationship on the x and y axes, respectively. True partnerships, characterized by highly aligned goals and a highly productive relationship, occupy the upper right corner of the matrix. The lower left corner, populated by pairs of institutions with opposing strategies and dysfunctional relationships, is home to the train wrecks. (See the illustration "How Well Do You Work with Grantees?" in this section.)

Getting a new relationship off to a good start is a great way to head toward the partnership quadrant. But, in actuality, you will always be pulling against harsh realities (and the forces of entropy) on the one hand, and the dynamics of making change on the other. Effective partnerships are built intentionally, over time. When circumstances change or new players join in, on either side of the relationship, there's a reservoir of goodwill to draw on. But if goodwill is taken for granted it will simply, and invisibly, melt away.

Meanwhile, shared goals, the strategic dimension of the matrix, tend to be even more dynamic, because implementation inevitably sparks learning, which in turn fosters strategic change. And if you are trying to do something that is even the smallest bit complicated, it's a virtual certainty that at least a few things won't turn out as anticipated. So unless you and your grantee can freely discuss what's going on, and adjust your strategies to evolving realities, your relationship will head in an unhappy and wasteful direction.

Philanthropy is not a popularity contest. Effective philanthropists must be disciplined and tough-minded about how they allocate their scarce resources. Yet it is also essential to be fair, to presume trust, and to earn trust. Demonstrating respect for the expertise and opinions of others, as well as for their time and resources, is critically important. Something as simple as promptly returning phone calls from grantees will go a long way toward keeping the lines of communication open, literally and figuratively.

Do good intentions automatically translate into impact? No. Do they vastly improve the odds of being able to engage

How well do you work with grantees?

Partnership: Regularly explore opportunities to build upon and leverage your successful partnership through innovative strategies, enhanced collaboration with other organizations and constituents, and increased financial and/or nonfinancial assistance.

Amiable Association: Actively clarify the strategic disconnects around goals and/or theories of change. Learn from one another; determine if overall results can be improved by more fully supporting the grantee's strategy—or by the grantee more actively embracing your strategy. Either accept the lost opportunities (and possible tensions) inherent in a lack of shared goals, or work together to align them.

Forced March: Identify practical opportunities to boost productivity through improved communication, better proposal and approval processes, more effective grant management, and useful reporting requirements. Simultaneously, pursue areas where you can add value to the grantee, such as mentoring, board development, program expertise, technical assistance, and fund-raising.

Train Wreck: Jointly confront the "brutal facts" of the situation. If constructive progress cannot be made to align the strategies better and/or improve the working relationship, then probably best to transition out.

in the kind of open, honest conversation required to achieve results, and to ensure that those results consistently improve over time? Yes. In the next (and final) chapter, we'll look at what it takes to apply a continuous-improvement mindset to your philanthropy.

6

AM I GETTING
BETTER?

THIS IS BOTH THE MOST POTENT OF OUR book's questions and the most challenging to answer. It's the most potent for two reasons: First, it focuses squarely on the results you're trying to achieve and demands that you have an informed point of view about your current performance. It's premised on the assumption that you can actually answer the question, "How am I really doing?" because you know what you are trying to accomplish, how your own efforts on that front are progressing, and where your grantees stand against the results you and they have agreed upon.

Second, it implies that whatever you're accomplishing with your philanthropy, however good the results, they could be better. "Am I getting better?" is a question about continuous improvement, not the status quo. It's the antithesis of the happy talk all too common in philanthropy, where performance discussions are like pass/fail courses, with pass equating to success and failure being highly unusual (and rarely discussed).

Whereas a pass/fail mindset lets decision makers off the hook for results and fosters chronic complacency, a "getting better" orientation acknowledges that performance is not so black and white, and that most of the time we fall short of what is possible. Conscientiously setting oneself to get better in philanthropy is basically no different than becoming better and better at one's profession, or working steadily to reduce one's golf handicap. Continuous learning compounds on itself, gradually providing higher "returns" for a given level of effort. By steadily learning to give smarter, you will be increasing your returns to society through the magic of compounding in much the same manner (albeit without the arithmetic certainty) that $100 at 5 percent interest will exceed $160 in ten years' time.

"Am I getting better?" is a challenging question, because it means confronting a basic, and uncomfortable, fact of life: getting better is a choice. When your doctor suggests adopting a healthier diet or exercising daily, you may decide to follow her advice . . . at least for a week or two. But getting healthier requires daily effort and constant personal discipline. Despite all manner of information and feedback, most people choose not to be healthy (until, perhaps, they suffer a heart attack or stroke!). Here, as in most circumstances, it takes a great deal of personal motivation to do the heavy lifting required to get better. Getting better in philanthropy is no exception to that rule.

Why take on this heavy lifting? In addition to the greater good it will generate for society, getting better can be good for you as well. "I want to do whatever is necessary to make my foundation 'best in class' given its size," the aging benefactor of a large family foundation recently told us. "Most foun-

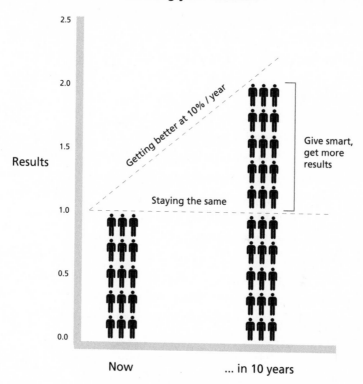

Is the magic of compounding increasing your results?

Results

2.5

2.0

1.5

1.0

0.5

0.0

Getting better at 10% / year

Staying the same

Give smart, get more results

Now

... in 10 years

dations do not achieve much; I want our family to stand out from the pack. My legacy is too important to do otherwise."[1]

Like this benefactor, many of the men and women now funding foundations have been winners in the highly competitive business arena. Striving to be "the best they can be" is a personal and deeply rooted motivation that carries over into their philanthropy. They want to leverage their resources, drive innovation, and take advantage of changing circumstances. They simply will not settle for "good enough."

If you are the steward of another person's money, you have an even greater responsibility to get better. Family members, trustees, and foundation executives have a moral duty to push themselves to do their best. Anything else undermines the legacy of the original donor, in addition to shortchanging society. Steve Hilton, grandson of Conrad Hilton and now president of the Conrad N. Hilton Foundation, knows the power of this responsibility.

"Conrad Hilton left a last will with clear guidelines as to what the foundation would do . . . that is not just a legal mandate, but a moral responsibility," he reflects.[2] Every board member signs a document acknowledging and committing to honor Conrad Hilton's intent to "relieve the suffering, the distressed, and the destitute."[3] Multiple foundation leaders have honored their duty to fulfill Conrad Hilton's dream, while also responding to the needs of their time.

Dodging the question "how do I get better?" is to accept the status quo which, eventually, will cause any endeavor to drift toward mediocrity. Philanthropy, on average, is just average—and given the lack of marketplace dynamics, the absence of competitors and paying customers, that average can be pretty low. Getting better—striving for excellence—is a fundamental choice. And deciding, courageously, to embrace that choice has one overarching central imperative: to learn.

LEARNING TO IMPROVE

Life offers many ways of getting lucky, but getting better, steadily better, requires learning. This is as true for philanthropists as it is for athletes, business executives, actors, and doctors. It applies to hobbies (improving a golf handicap) and to our personal lives (learning to be a good parent). When people and organizations become set in their ways, as a result of arrogance or closed-mindedness, they stifle real learning. Entire industries, like U.S. auto manufacturing, have fallen into this trap. And we all know individuals who seemed to stop learning in their thirties or forties. Learning requires a certain degree of humility, recognition, and acknowledgment of what you may not know or may have gotten wrong, as well as the resolve to invest the time and energy to steadily improve.

When you're intent on getting better, not all learning is created equal. In fact, it's easy to become distracted by information that looks interesting but is not necessarily germane (there is, after all, a seemingly limitless supply of data and competing points of view). The most useful learning will come from information that helps you make smarter decisions: about your strategy (which issues and organizations to fund and with how much money, for example), and about how it can be executed more effectively (whether to strengthen a key grantee's organizational or financial capacity, for instance, or where to invest your personal time in building relationships with key stakeholders, a decision that always requires tough trade-offs).

It should come as no surprise, then, that your grantees are likely to be the source of much of this useful information, since the success of your philanthropy is largely dependent on their results. Because of this interdependence, virtually every grant of any size will include a requirement for regular updates and progress reports. Increasingly, what grant makers want to see in those reports are quantitative data that can be tracked over time to demonstrate results, or the lack thereof. One benefactor we know puts it this way:

"I've worked my tail off for decades, created a lot of jobs, earned a lot of money and paid a lot of taxes . . . I don't owe society a nickel. But boy, do I give a lot of nickels away! My philanthropy is a voluntary investment I make in the service of future generations, for the world my kids and their kids will grow up in. If people like me, with my resources and my good fortune, don't choose to step forward to serve society, then who will? I don't need philanthropic accolades, but I do demand that my hard-earned money be put to good use. I demand visible results from the nickels I give away."[4]

The challenge is that the growing focus on results has also generated a certain amount of confusion and inconsistency about what to measure, when, and how. Social impact can be defiantly difficult to quantify, and beleaguered nonprofit leaders have dozens if not hundreds of tools competing for their attention. For their part, many donors compound the confusion by aggressively imposing their own specific measures on grantees, without stopping to ask exactly how the resulting data would add value.

Does this mean giving up on measurement? Not in the least. But it does mean being thoughtful, and working with your grantees to understand what measures they, and you, think could best inform the strategic and operational decisions they have to make. To paraphrase Mario Morino, a founder of Venture Philanthropy Partners, and one of the most knowledgeable and thoughtful philanthropists we know, measurement is a means to an end, not an end in and of itself. The end is helping nonprofits create greater benefits for the people and causes they serve. That, in turn, requires "gaining real clarity on the change we are trying to create . . . figuring out what information is most helpful for determining how we're doing, and using this information to guide our key decisions and actions."[5]

LEARNING WITH, AND FROM, GRANTEES

In the world of nonprofits and NGOs, measurement serves three quite different purposes: accountability (what did our donors get for their money?); continuous improvement (given these results, and what we now know, how can we get better?); and proof of impact (can the results we're seeing really be tied to the work our organization did?). Consequently, engaging effectively with your grantees around measurement begins with being clear about the "why"; that is, which of these three purposes you're trying to address.

When you assess your grantee's performance with accountability in the foreground, you're basically focusing on keeping score. It is the philanthropic equivalent of a final exam, where the real question is "Have you delivered the results I'm paying you to deliver?" Scorekeeping is essentially backward looking: it tells you what happened, but not necessarily why it happened, or how to improve next time. It is necessary, but not sufficient, if you and your grantees are jointly committed to seeing their results improve.

In contrast, when you approach measurement as a vehicle for learning and improvement, it becomes more like a diagnostic or placement exam. The objective here is to understand not only what the organization has done, but also what its strengths and weaknesses are, and what it might need to change going forward. In this case, you're less like a score-keeper than a coach. Measuring for learning and improvement is akin to what the business world knows as "performance management": collecting ongoing quantitative and qualitative data about an organization's programs and activities, so that its leadership can make better decisions in real time.

When you're managing for outcomes, the information you gather provides a point of departure for learning, adaptation, and innovation. It is inherently forward looking, and helps to illuminate how programs can improve, how beneficiaries can be better served, and whether an organization's theory of change is playing out as anticipated.

The third reason to measure—measuring to ascertain proof of impact—has attracted a great deal of attention in recent years, as both philanthropists and government funders have become increasingly interested in funding what works. An impact evaluation is a one-time assessment, designed to provide evidence that a specific program has created a hoped-for change. It seeks to answer questions about causality that performance management cannot address. For example, if a goodly number of the participants in an inner-city job-training program succeed in finding employment, an impact evaluation will try to determine whether their success is attributable to the program, or whether other factors (such as a resurgent local economy) were at play.

Perhaps the best-known form of impact evaluation is a randomized controlled trial (RCT), a type of scientific experiment that originated in medicine. It avoids selection bias by randomly assigning individuals to receive services, or not (thereby creating a control group). RCTs and other forms of impact evaluation are appropriate and valuable for certain organizations, at certain points in their development. For example, a nonprofit that has codified its program and achieved great results in one state might require an impact evaluation before seeking private and/or government funding to move to national scale. But whereas every organization needs measures that can help it improve, the number of nonprofits that would benefit from some sort of rigorous and costly impact evaluation is actually fairly small.

Once you've clarified the "why" of measurement, you're ready to reflect on the "what": the information you and/or your grantees actually need in order to learn and improve. Although the particulars will vary from case to case, we're willing to bet that the measures that emerge as genuinely useful will be strategic, situational, and actionable.

The most important measures are those that *inform strategy*. Recall that a theory of change is just that: a theory. Theories are fundamentally your best guess, and in a dynamic world theories are rarely perfect. They are always grounded in a set of assumptions about the context and behavior of others, assumptions that require testing and can quickly become outdated. You will not deliver results (much less get better) if the nonprofits and initiatives you fund are not strategically robust.

Second, the right measures are *situational*. The measures that will help you improve your philanthropy will depend on your needs and your grantee's stage of development. If you're making a long-term financial commitment to a new and relatively risky initiative (such as funding a remedial program for juvenile dropouts or working to reduce urban poverty), multiple measures are probably essential to test and refine your theory of change. In contrast, if you're funding the purchase of conservation lands or making a large contribution to your alma mater, you may decide you don't need any measures at all.

Your grantees' circumstances will also dictate different measurement needs and approaches: the nascent and unproven after-school program for dropouts needs basic measures to assess its early outcomes and refine its program model; the well-established conservation organization with a proven strategy may benefit more from measures that can help it scale or replicate.

Finally, the right measures will be *actionable*. The basic premise of this book is that philanthropists making smarter decisions achieve better results. This means the measures that matter are the ones that inform and improve decisions. If you cannot connect a given measure to a decision that you (or your grantee) need to make, it's probably unnecessary.

SUPPORTING YOUR GRANTEES' CONTINUOUS IMPROVEMENT

Individuals and organizations tend to learn from two distinctly different experiences: what works well, and what does not work so well. Failure, in fact, is often a better teacher than success. Yet most of us find it discomforting to accept our shortcomings, much less to acknowledge them explicitly to others. So we accentuate the positive, while ignoring the negative (or what management expert Jim Collins refers to as the "brutal facts"[6]). In so doing, we limit our ability to improve.

Philanthropy creates an almost ideal setting for this sort of avoidance and self-deception. Grantees have little incentive to take the initiative in reporting "mistakes" to donors, lest they diminish their reputation and jeopardize future funding. It isn't that they intentionally try to deceive their funders; just that, at the margin, good news is more likely to flow than bad news.

Donors, on the other hand, want to know that their contributions made a difference. They are not uniformly inclined to be rigorous about exploring where their funds might have been "wasted." This dynamic is particularly prevalent in larger established foundations where program officers must be effective internal advocates to secure their grant budgets. All the while, shared passion creates an inclination to believe, to hope for the best no matter what the data may indicate. As a consequence of these very human dynamics, flawed nonprofit strategies and poor execution can persist well beyond any reasonable time frame.

Given these realities, how you approach conversations about performance with your grantees will send an important signal as to whether you want to hear the whole truth, or only the good news. Assuming you're more interested in being a coach than a referee, the best way to signal that intention is by asking the right questions in a spirit of partnership.

What are the right questions? Basically they're the same ones you'd use to assess your own performance: "What are the results you're trying to achieve?" "What is your strategy for achieving them?" (In other words, what is your theory of change?) And "What is the information you need in order to test your theory of change?" The objective is to help both of you understand where they are making progress, where they may need to improve (programmatically or organizationally), and where there might be opportunities to innovate.

Questions like these can be particularly helpful when, as may often be the case, the nonprofits or NGOs you're funding don't yet have good measurement systems in place. The reason is that they demonstrate the link between measurement and mission. Measurement has the potential to be a daunting challenge. Experience shows that when an organization's leaders really understand how good data can help them improve outcomes for those they serve, it is much more readily embraced.

Working with grantees to develop measurement systems that will help them make their most important strategic and operational decisions also means that the data they track are likely to be relevant for other donors as well. Most nonprofits have multiple funders. If each of those funders establishes his or her own set of critical metrics, the nonprofit's cost of capital will escalate, while the chances of actually gleaning useful information will plummet. So if the organizations you're supporting do have good measurement systems already in place, listen to what they propose, and think hard before inventing new measures for them.

Most important, you can support your grantees' learning and continuous improvement by not being cheap. In chapter 4, we discussed the critical capacity issues that nonprofits face. If most nonprofits struggle to find staff and time to accomplish basic operational tasks, like performance reviews for personnel and ongoing financial planning, consider how likely it is that measurement will look like a "nice to have," not a "need to have" activity. For most nonprofits, measurement can feel like an added cost burden on an already overfilled plate. Yet for them and for you to achieve ever better results, measurement is essential. As a donor, you can add significant value simply by helping them develop the capacity to do it.

Most donors, as we've seen, shy away from paying for overhead. Where learning is concerned, this becomes an especially acute problem. If donors are unwilling to provide adequate resources to develop prototypes, test ideas, solicit feedback, and measure effectiveness, much less invest to recruit and develop a capable organization, it is like having a high-performing car with no gas in the tank. You just won't go very far. Provide the funds for systems that can help collect and compare data. Be open to needs for new staff to oversee measurement efforts. Getting better will cost money, but it is money that can be spent to generate huge returns.

AM I BECOMING A BETTER PHILANTHROPIST?

A few years ago, a private equity friend of ours was bragging to his wife about the windfall he had just earned thanks to a portfolio company's initial private offering. "Honey," she responded, "just because you're rich, doesn't mean you're smart." Her candid feedback was a reminder that achievement is nurtured in the arms of humility, not arrogance. The implication for philanthropy: having money is not the same as having answers. Without regularly asking yourself the question "Am I getting better?" you will most assuredly underperform your potential.

For Connie Duckworth, philanthropy has been an ongoing and at times all-consuming learning journey. After retiring from Goldman Sachs, where she was the first woman to become a sales and trading partner, she was invited to join the Department of State's U.S.-Afghan Women's Council, designed, as she describes it, "to make sure women have a seat at the table in the new Afghanistan."[7] Already an engaged philanthropist, the experience opened her eyes to a new passion. "Going there and seeing the conditions of these women, prompted me to act. After my first trip I said, 'I'm doing something,' even though I had no idea what the something would be."

In light of Duckworth's belief that economic empowerment gives women control of their own destiny, it's not surprising that "something" became a nonprofit social enterprise, called Arzu from the Dari word for "hope."[8] Initially inclined to focus Arzu on garment making, she quickly discovered that the work was ill suited to the conditions and norms of the country. For one thing, the women would be unable to leave their family compounds, even if a factory were to be built. What did fit was rug making, a traditional, home-based occupation for women.

By learning from on-the-ground insights like this, as well as from the efforts of others, Duckworth has helped Arzu become one of the largest private employers of women in Afghanistan. She has built a grassroots business that is thriving where most other economic development projects are failing. (Rug sales already cover 45 percent of Arzu's costs.) She has also tied jobs to education and health, particularly maternal and infant care. All the children in employees' families who are under fifteen must be in school, for example, while all the women must attend local literacy classes. In a country with the highest lifetime risk of mortality in the world (the odds that a fifteen-year-old girl will eventually die from maternal causes are one in eleven[9]), none of the women in Arzu's care have died in childbirth. And, last but not least, Arzu has become a learning laboratory for grassroots, sustainable development as well as a pioneering model for what the military and others are beginning to call "expeditionary economics."

What has the impact on Duckworth herself been? In her words, "Incredible . . . This effort has opened me to an entire new network of interesting people, in walks of life I would never have encountered in my Goldman traffic pattern— people in the development world, and scientists, designers, marines and the economics department at West Point. It is incredibly nourishing personally as well as intellectually. Looking at the impact you can have on other people's lives and on some of these 'intractable' problems, even if the impact is small, it's real, and it's just tremendous."

Philanthropists intent on continuous improvement cast a wide net for information that can help them make better decisions. They attend conferences, read, and consult Web sites in order to learn from experts and others engaged in supporting or working on the issues they care about. They help build new knowledge, by funding pilots and experiments, commissioning research, and sharing the findings. They solicit feedback about their own performance from their grantees, directly and anonymously (through surveys like those conduced by the Center for Effective Philanthropy). Equally important, they get out into the field to understand the context for their work and to listen to those they aim to serve.

But it is also true that whether you are giving through a donor-advised fund, making grants through a private family foundation, or leading a large foundation with paid staff, the time required to do the work will always vastly outweigh the time available for improving it. This is a law of nature as applicable to individual donors as it is to hundred-person foundations. The harsh Monday-morning reality is that there will never, ever be enough time to get everything done. Consultants, academics, experts, and pundits may offer elegant insights about improving your philanthropy, but they don't have to walk that talk. Most days in the real world, "keeping up" and "catching up" take precedence over "getting better."

At the risk of oversimplification, therefore, we recommend focusing one's efforts at improvement around two critical questions: "Do the results of my philanthropy equal the success I aspire to see?" and "Am I using my scarce resources wisely?"

IS MY STRATEGY ON TRACK?

For donors whose major philanthropic activity is giving money to qualified nonprofit organizations, the primary imperative around improvement (as we've previously discussed) is to get better at selecting, funding, and supporting grantees. When you and your grantees have the same definition of success, your performance scorecard is their record of results. If you support a local K-8 charter school, for example, and the success you aspire to see is a 100 percent graduation rate, the number of graduates each year will tell you precisely how your philanthropy is doing. Similarly, if you're defining success as the preservation of a thousand acres of salt marsh, and you fund a project at The Nature Conservancy to do just that, you will succeed if they do.

But suppose your definition of success (per chapter 2) encompasses more than these individual organizations or projects. What if your real aim is to transform your local school district, or preserve the entire estuary? In circumstances like these, your grantees may be achieving the desired results, but you may not be achieving success.

This distinction is not simply semantic. When the results you're currently holding yourself accountable for are one part of a larger whole, you also need to see what's happening elsewhere, so that you can test whether the assumptions and hypotheses embedded in the theory of change driving your strategy still make sense. In short, you need to learn. And the upshot may be discovering that you need to adapt your course, as the Gill Foundation did in its pursuit of equal rights for all Americans.

Tim Gill is the founder of Quark, the Denver-based software company, and a gay man. In 1992, Coloradans passed Amendment 2, a ballot initiative denying equal protection under the law to lesbians and gays. Although the U.S. Supreme Court ultimately struck down the amendment, Gill decided to raise awareness, in his home state and across the nation, around gay rights. In 1994, he established the Gill Foundation, which is now one of the largest funders of lesbian, gay, bisexual, and transgender (LGBT) civil rights work.[10]

One of the foundation's strategies focused on promoting the adoption of legislation at the state level outlawing hate crimes. After years of work and the passage of several new state laws, however, they learned that the legislation wasn't actually reducing the incidence of these crimes. Strong enforcement, with the cooperation of police and prosecutors, was needed to drive real change.[11] In response, the foundation shifted its strategy to emphasize enforcement. Gains have already been achieved in several states: overall, since 2000, hate crime incidents against LGBT individuals are down 22 percent.[12] That said, the initial strategy was far from a failure, since effective enforcement would be impossible were legislation not on the books.

The more unknowns your theory of change involves, the more important it is to test and, if need be, update the hypotheses embedded in it. The David and Lucile Packard Foundation's practices illustrate the way that regularly revisiting your theory of change can be the catalyst for making real progress against a critically important issue.

Conserving and restoring the earth's natural systems is one of the cornerstones of the Packard Foundation's philanthropy.[13] To that end, its marine fisheries program focuses on improving the health of the planet's oceans and wild fish stocks. As part of this effort, in 1999 Packard launched Seafood Choices, an initiative intended to increase the demand for, and supply of, sustainable seafood. Because there was little (if any) hard evidence about what would have to happen to achieve those results, Packard spent the first several years seeding experiments. They ranged from campaigns to persuade chefs and consumers to avoid over-fished species to encouraging fishermen around the world to adopt more sustainable practices.

Packard's leadership has long regarded a commitment to learning and continuous improvement as part of their legacy from David Packard, and the culture and practices he nurtured at Hewlett-Packard. So, in 2004, they took a step back to evaluate their early efforts and revisit their strategy. They read scores of media, market, and funding reports. They sought insights from key industry players, researchers, and academics. One of the things they learned was that sustainability was becoming the focus of increasing global attention, especially among large seafood retailers. Armed with this new information, Packard examined its portfolio of marine-conservation grants. It decided to cut back on its awareness campaigns, which seemed to be having little immediate, direct effect on individual consumer behavior, and redouble its efforts to influence these very large buyers.[14]

In 2007, the foundation engaged in another round of research, reflection, and reevaluation. Interest in sustainability among retailers was still rising; for example, in 2006 Wal-Mart announced a commitment to sourcing sustainable seafood for its stores. But, as before, the findings both affirmed the value of existing efforts and pointed to new needs, among them the need to enlist wholesale suppliers and processors (who link fishermen with the buyers of their catch) more fully into the sustainability effort.[15]

Some grant makers take a fresh look at their strategies on a regular basis (every three to five years, say). For others, the trigger is an abrupt change in the context in which their strategy is unfolding. Shifts in funding and government legislation, breakthroughs in science or technology, and changes in public attitudes can all provoke an ambitious donor to hit the refresh button. In the past few years, such catalysts have been evident in fields ranging from health care to education to the environment. Old philanthropic strategies in these fields are very likely to be obsolete strategies.

AM I ALLOCATING
MY RESOURCES WISELY?

Just as testing and refining your overarching theory of change is an essential dimension of continuous improvement, so is a disciplined and clear-minded approach to resource allocation. In philanthropy, as in traditional investing, resource allocation decisions are enormously important in determining the performance of your portfolio. The relative size of specific grant commitments, their duration, and whether the grants are unrestricted or restricted will all contribute to determining your cumulative philanthropic "return on investment." Yet we know from firsthand experience that these decisions can be driven as much by personal whim, internal politics, and random events as by any form of rigorous and disciplined thought. Consider a few examples.

At a dinner party, a donor's friend aggressively pitches him on the problem of obesity among American schoolchildren. Swept up by his friend's passion, the donor subsequently proposes to the board of his foundation that they give his friend's nonprofit a major gift. The foundation has been focused for years on issues related to family homelessness, and has no experience whatsoever with anything related to health care. Nevertheless, despite modest grumbling and with essentially no analysis, the board approves the grant.

A family foundation executive acknowledges a grantee's need for $1 million to finance an initiative with the potential to create significantly better outcomes for the participants, but insists they launch it with only $100,000. Eager to test the promising new approach, the nonprofit goes ahead, despite the $900,000 shortfall, which they are unable to compensate for in the near term. Given the inadequate resources, the results are disappointing. Now convinced that the initiative was a bad idea in the first place, the donor backs off, causing the promising effort to shut down.

A large foundation giving away more than $10 million a year has hundreds of active grantees across four continents, addressing an array of issues from global warming to bicycle safety in Viet Nam. The average grant commitment? Less than $75,000, with a duration of less than eighteen months.

These anonymous but all too true anecdotes represent three of the most common resource allocation pitfalls philanthropists are apt to fall into: blind love, wrong sizing, and peanut butter philanthropy. When you're making a decision, blind love will encourage you to let your heart outdistance your brain (a problem certainly not confined to philanthropy!). Without the benefit of the clear-eyed thinking we have advocated throughout this book, it can also allow personal agendas to eclipse strategic priorities. Wrong sizing all too often causes unintended harm, because it fails to provide the resources actually required to "get the job done." Peanut butter philanthropy spreads resources so thinly that they are essentially wasted. There is nothing inherently wrong with small grants when they are applied to small problems. But when the problem to be solved is larger than the grant, such grants almost always fail to add up to any meaningful results (especially when compared with your aspirations).

Even the most conscientious donors fall into these resource allocation traps from time to time. The imperative is to be self-disciplined and strategic enough in one's decision making to resist these natural impulses.

How you manage your time, and your relationships with the world outside your doors, are also resource allocation decisions. In addition to building productive grantee relationships, how effectively are you interacting with other donors, government organizations, experts, and leaders in your areas of interest? Do you have productive relationships characterized by mutual respect? Are you learning from those with more experience? Are you benefiting fully from the organizations, people, and ideas outside your institution and your grantee base? Or are you confined to your silo, broadcasting your perspectives and strategies to others, and waiting (usually in vain) for them to respond to your brilliant plans?

As a rule, philanthropists overestimate their personal influence, while underestimating what others in their field already know. This creates two problems: relying on people to behave in ways that seldom materialize (providing money for initiatives they don't lead, for example); and reinventing the wheel and making avoidable mistakes, because others' experience and existing knowledge are ignored.

Learning happens through interactions. Tapping into the extended knowledge of other individuals and organizations can greatly leverage your efforts. Yet too many donors insist on going it alone. This truth was driven home to us when a particularly inexperienced (but highly confident) philanthropist proclaimed flatly: "I've met dozens of leaders in the education field, and there is not a single thing I can learn from any of them." Attitudes like his undercut both influence and learning, which is especially problematic if your strategy requires the cooperation of others to achieve success.

WHO ARE MY TRUTH TELLERS?

Achieving excellence requires useful learning which, in turn, is driven by timely feedback—a postulate as true for individuals as it is for organizations. What does it take to access the kind of feedback that will fuel learning and promote continuous improvement? The answer, in short, is truth telling.

Truth telling penetrates the egos, misperceptions, wishful thinking, ambiguity, and isolation of philanthropy. It is the single most essential input for a donor committed to continuous improvement—and it can easily be drowned out by philanthropy's dynamic but pernicious blend of money, power, and strong personalities. Unless you aggressively pursue the truth, you most assuredly will not find it. Happy talk will dominate at the expense of candor. The voices willing to tell you what isn't working, as well as what is, will fade away amid the din of self-congratulation.

Truth telling begins at home. Your day-to-day behavior—as donor, trustee, or foundation executive—will signal to your colleagues whether you are really open to hearing problems, or whether you prefer being told what they think you want to hear. Sandy Weill, the founder and board chair of National Academy Foundation (NAF) and the former CEO of Citigroup, often attends staff retreats to build personal relationships with NAF's leadership. And he just as regularly asks whether senior people feel able to take risks. As JD Hoye, NAF's president reports, "Sandy knows . . . that innovations are thwarted by a lack of risk taking. And he realizes that for every home run there are dozens of strikeouts. So the key is how you manage the strikeouts to learn."[16]

Everyone, of course, says they are open minded, but their

actions don't always square with their words. When was the last time you personally solicited and received "constructive" feedback? Do people come to you to discuss problems, or do you see only prepackaged solutions? Are your meetings a balance of inquiry and advocacy, or just people pushing their points of view? Do you really want to hear candid feedback, no matter how awkward or painful?

Jeff Raikes's answer to this last question is a resounding yes. As CEO of the world's largest foundation, he knows quite well how hard it can be to get candid feedback. However, he also knows that the Gates Foundation cannot succeed without it, because "the bigger the challenges and the more ambiguous the solutions, the more you need to hear a wide variety of viewpoints to innovate and learn."[17] And as Raikes sees it, the Gates Foundation is most definitely in the "innovation business," continually on the watch for successful ideas that can be shared and transferred to raise the standard of life for people around the globe.

To this end, he has sought to create feedback loops and to identify truth tellers in a variety of ways. Shortly after coming on board, for example, Raikes asked the Center for Effective Philanthropy to survey all the foundation's grantees. When the report came back, it revealed considerable dissatisfaction with the way the foundation made decisions, communicated with grantees, and explained its strategies and goals. Instead of suppressing the criticisms, Raikes wrote them up in his annual letter (which he posted on the foundation's Web site), along with a set of action steps for getting better.[18]

He has been equally active and forthright about reaching out to employees (who reported similar feelings of frustration with foundation decision making), to independent experts in fields the foundation funds, and to journalists who have been critical of the foundation in their columns and articles. "I may not agree with everything they say," Raikes notes. "But it is important to understand how they see the world and to factor it into our thinking."

Truth telling also embraces failure. To improve, donors must learn from mistakes, yet in philanthropy "failure" is like the crazy uncle people whisper about but rarely acknowledge. The same philanthropists who tout "risk taking" and "innovation" often go silent when asked to describe their failures. Part of the reason for this, they claim, is to protect the innocent (usually grantees). But something more fundamental is going on. Donors basically don't like acknowledging failure—to themselves, in their board room, or among their colleagues and staff. In dozens of interviews with philanthropists, we found only a handful of individuals willing to discuss examples of failure, even off the record.

It doesn't help that simple-minded media reports tend to call any effort short of perfection a failure, regardless of the value the initiative actually creates. Labeling something a failure begs the question: a failure relative to what? To doing nothing? To not trying in the first place? Since we have not cured cancer, this logic would suggest that the billions of dollars of philanthropic (and public sector) funding committed to cancer research has "failed," an unlikely conclusion in the minds of most people. Treating failure as an absolute also inhibits public disclosure of philanthropic "failures" which, in turn, suppresses knowledge sharing and learning.

Acknowledging the reality that most results are not binary and that learning occurs from all manner of shortfalls, some innovative grant makers are pushing ahead in defense of failure. The Robert Wood Johnson Foundation has published an annual volume for more than a decade that includes lessons learned from unsuccessful initiatives, while the William and Flora Hewlett Foundation is one of a number of leading foundations that post their so-called failures on their Web sites. Hewlett CEO Paul Brest and his team also engage in "worst decision" competitions just to reinforce a truth-telling culture.[19]

In the end, truth telling requires truth tellers: courageous people who will risk telling you exactly how they see things, even when the message is tough and unwelcome. You need truth tellers on your board and in your organization, and among your grantees and your external advisors. Truth tellers won't necessarily agree, and they can't be counted upon to have answers, but they will have honest points of view that will help you get to answers that will enable your philanthropy to adapt, innovate, and draw closer to achieving success.

WHY NOW?

If there was ever a time for philanthropists to step forward and give smart, it is now. The convergence of powerful forces has been building for over a decade. It is fueling innovation as well as a focus on impact across the social sector. Many of the stories and voices in this book reflect the dynamic optimism of our era. Donors are attracting new leaders, funding new experiments, developing new insights, and challenging old models. Many are using technology to drive their theories of change, or to accelerate the creation and distribution of knowledge. With increasing evidence of the potential for effective collaboration, the boundaries between business, government, and nonprofits are blurring. Innovation in philanthropy is not new: the twentieth century had more than its share of success stories. What is new is the scale and momentum of the innovation, propelled by the twin resources of money and talent.

Much has been made of America's historic "wealth transfer," the intergenerational flow of funds into philanthropy likely to occur in coming decades, as a result of the wealth and longevity of the members of the baby boom generation.[20] Benefiting from America's post–World War II prosperity, these men and women grew up in a stable and affluent era. They inherited wealth from the "greatest generation," to which their parents belonged, and also created an absolutely unprecedented amount of wealth in their own right. And as Peter Drucker pointed out decades ago, advances in health care have allowed them to lead productive lives well beyond the life spans of prior generations. Instead of retiring at age sixty-five, they are more inclined to reorient themselves around new careers. In a sense, boomers are the "lucky generation," born at an opportune time and place in history, and now disproportionately blessed with abundant resources and the time to use them wisely.

In the summer of 2010, Warren Buffett and Bill and Melinda Gates challenged fellow billionaires to commit to giving at least half their wealth to society, during their lives and/or through a foundation after their deaths.[21] Within three months, some forty others pledged publicly to do just that. We believe these events are indicators of what lies in store for society. As Andrew Carnegie pointed out in his essay the "Gospel of Wealth," a personal fortune can go to the government in the form of taxes, to one's children (which, he asserted, would spoil both them and their offspring), or to society in the form of philanthropy. Those three options are the same today as they were in 1889. The difference is that philanthropy seems to be gaining share.

Research indicates that the amount of funds flowing into foundations during the first half of the twenty-first century will be ten times that of the entire twentieth century (after adjusting for inflation).[22] That is ten times the money in half the time! While none of us can predict the future economic trends that will influence the ultimate net worth of the world's donors, there is no denying that whether the figure is five times, ten times, or even more, an unprecedented amount of wealth is destined for the social sector in the decades ahead.

Less discussed, but of even more significance, is America's talent transfer. Philanthropists are investing their own time as well as their treasure to drive results. When an entrepreneur as wealthy and successful as Bill Gates leaves his executive position at age fifty to devote his full energies to his philanthropy, it is a signature event for society. Countless others are similarly inspiring role models.

But the talent transfer is not even remotely confined to wealthy philanthropists. Teach for America is now the largest recruiter at several Ivy League colleges and major universities. In some cases it has attracted applications from over 10 percent of graduating seniors.[23] Among older Americans, the appeal of encore careers is motivating those in their fifties, sixties, and seventies to engage in public service, through both volunteer and paid positions. People of every age are stepping forward to donate their scarce hours to communities and causes they care about—a far more precious and limited resource than any philanthropist's money.

The motivation to serve has many manifestations. For instance, one recent study concluded that over 20 percent of all nonprofit senior executives have transitioned directly from the business sector.[24] As nonprofit organizations get larger, they're also actively seeking to develop future generations of star talent from within and across the sector. All these various talent flows drive innovation by providing new ideas, new energy, and new leadership to leverage philanthropic dollars. To deliver results, talent needs money and money needs talent. The abundance of both these resources creates an unprecedented opportunity for society. The challenge of "getting better" is ensuring that this opportunity is not squandered, and that donors and foundation executives strive relentlessly for results, learning, and innovation.

WHY ME?

The journey from philanthropic aspirations to real impact is anything but easy. Whether you are a donor, a trustee, or a foundation executive, you confront complex challenges, tough decisions, and problems that can seem resolutely resistant to being solved. Your resources are limited in comparison to what you're striving to achieve. And because you're almost always working with and through others, you can exert precious little control over how things ultimately play out. Common sense would seem to dictate taking an easier path, to skip the hard questions and just allow yourself to feel good giving money away.

That would be a loss, for you as well as for society. Other people (including generations yet unborn) are counting on you to do your very best, to impose excellence on yourself and those around you, by working to make every dollar and every hour yield the greatest possible results. As you have seen in these pages, more and more philanthropists are signing on to that imperative.

When we talk with successful people about their accomplishments, they invariably say that they consider themselves lucky. They insist that some sort of luck—the families they were born into, the serendipity of career decisions, aspects of their personal life—played a central role in their success. The fundamental belief that "I drew aces and the other guy didn't" has motivated donors, from Andrew Carnegie onward, to aim high in the service of others less fortunate than themselves.

So "why me?" Your philanthropy—the results you are holding yourself accountable for achieving—is focused on the people and communities and causes you aspire to serve. It is about them, not you. And yet in another, deeper sense, your philanthropy is indeed all about you. Whether you are giving away your money or you are a steward of another's money, your philanthropy is fundamentally about your values, your life, and your legacy. How you approach your philanthropy offers the most unfiltered manifestation of who you really are as a human being. Generous or selfish. Wise or naive. Humble or arrogant. Smart or impulsive. For better or worse, philanthropy is a defining act, one that can generate immense joy and a deep sense of personal fulfillment.

We wish you luck and Godspeed in your journey.

A MONDAY MORNING CHECKLIST

The questions posed in this book aren't the kind you ask, and answer, once and for all. On the contrary, the odds are that you'll find yourself coming back to one or more of them at various points (and in various combinations) throughout your philanthropic journey. And yet, you can't ask questions forever; sooner or later you must make decisions. So how can you tell whether you've wrestled with a question sufficiently to move on? In our experience, each of these questions has some relatively clear indicators of progress. If you can check many of these markers off your Monday morning to-do list, then you're probably well on your way to giving smart!

"WHAT ARE MY VALUES AND BELIEFS?"

You've decided what portion of your philanthropy will focus explicitly on results.

You've written down your values and beliefs.

You've discussed your values and beliefs with your spouse, family, and, if appropriate, your foundation leadership.

The people most relevant to your giving know what you do, and do not, care about.

You have anchor points for your current philanthropic initiatives.

If you've been at this for a while, you've stepped back at least once to test how well your values are informing your philanthropic decisions.

"WHAT IS 'SUCCESS' AND HOW CAN IT BE ACHIEVED?"

Your definition of success is clear enough to allow you, and others, to judge progress against it.

You can specify the key assumptions that underlie your theory of change.

You've taken the time to learn what others know about the essential elements of your theory of change.

Knowledgeable outsiders (including experts in your chosen field) think your theory of change is worth pursuing.

All the decision makers involved in your philanthropy (including trustees and staff if relevant) understand and embrace your definition of success and theory of change.

Your theory of change, not ad hoc interests or unsolicited requests, is driving funding decisions.

If you've been pursuing your theory of change for several years, you've revisited your initial thinking at least once and asked what is, and is not, working as you expected.

"WHAT AM I ACCOUNTABLE FOR?"

You've been explicit with yourself and others about how
much money, time, and influence you're prepared to commit to a specific initiative.

Impartial but knowledgeable observers would say that the resources you intend to contribute are proportional to your
strategy and the success you aspire to achieve.

You've explicitly considered and accepted the risks (strategic,
secondary, and personal) associated with your strategy.

You've been crystal clear about what you are *not* doing.

Other people describe you as a donor who "walks the talk"
and honors commitments: you hold yourself accountable.

"WHAT WILL IT TAKE TO GET THE JOB DONE?"

You're confident that you have the right people, in the right
jobs, to pursue your strategy; if not, you're actively addressing the problem.

You and your trustees and staff usually agree on important
decisions; when you disagree, a candid discussion ensues,
and people come together around the ultimate decision.

Trustees and staff understand their roles and decision-making
responsibilities.

Trustees enjoy coming to board meetings, because they know
their contributions are substantive and valued.

Your grantees would say that you are realistic about the resources they need to execute their strategies.

Your own organization has the resources it requires to execute your strategy.

If you have been at this for a while, you've periodically reassessed whether you and your grantees have the capacity required to get the job done.

"HOW DO I WORK WITH GRANTEES?"

You invest in due diligence to ensure that your selection process is as rigorous as the circumstances of the grant require.

Organizations you turn down for funding would say they were treated fairly and with respect.

You and your grantees have shared goals; if asked "What's an 'A'?" you would have similar answers.

Your grantees would select you over other donors, all else being equal.

Grantees trust you enough to come to you, unsolicited, with serious problems.

Organizations you've ceased to fund would say you ended the relationship as thoughtfully as you began it.

You have a reputation for following the Golden Rule in your philanthropy: you treat others as you yourself would want to be treated.

"AM I GETTING BETTER?"

You can judge (even if you can't measure) whether you, and your grantees, are making progress toward your goals.

You cast a wide net externally for information relevant to your fields of interest.

Your grantees would say that as a donor you help them get better.

You periodically seek feedback from your grantees about your own performance, including in ways that ensure their anonymity.

You can name one (or more) grants that didn't work out as hoped and have shared the lessons you learned with others.

You're in regular contact with at least a few people who challenge your thinking.

Over time, your philanthropy generates real results on society's behalf: the people and/or the issues that you and your grantees seek to serve are clearly better off.

WITH GRATITUDE

With books, as in philanthropy, little can be accomplished alone. Results are achieved through collaboration and by building upon existing knowledge. *Give Smart* is no exception to this rule. From first to last, the contributions of an extraordinary group of colleagues, friends, advisors, and thinkers have helped to shape and sharpen its content. It is, truly, the work of many hands and minds.

Allison Murphy's careful research provided a wealth of contemporary illustrations to complement Joel's historical examples. Her rigor, thoughtful insights, and drafting prowess greatly enhanced the manuscript at many points, while her powers of coordination, even temperament, and quick smile helped us navigate all manner of speed bumps. She was, in a word, indispensable.

Susan Wolf Ditkoff served as thought leader extraordinaire. A Bridgespan partner with extensive experience consulting to and advising philanthropists, Susan not only kept us focused and lucid, but also ensured that we incorporated relevant lessons from Bridgespan's decade of work with donors and the nonprofits they support.

Katie Smith Milway, the head of Bridgespan's knowledge efforts, led the book's development process, from the original conversations with PublicAffairs through to the final copy. An accomplished author and experienced executive in her own right, she provided a stream of advice and suggestions that were invaluable.

Many other Bridgespan partners generously contributed time as well as ideas to help us strengthen and improve *Give Smart*'s content. Managing Director Jeff Bradach was a tireless champion and relentless reader of our work in process. William Foster, Don

Howard, Richard Steele, Jeri Eckhart-Queenan, Kirk Kramer, Alan Tuck, Kelly Campbell, Margaret Boasberg, and Susan Colby all shared insights and examples from their consulting work, research, and writing. Whenever we needed them, they were there for us, demonstrating Bridgespan's values: impact, respect, candor, collaboration, and passion.

In writing this book, we set out to capture philanthropy's "timeless truths"—the few essential questions and related ideas that would help donors, and the organizations they fund, achieve the best possible results. So it should come as no surprise that the work of others, in both business and the social sector, has been instrumental in shaping our thinking. Perhaps no single individual was more influential than Jim Collins; his work became a cornerstone for much of our approach, while his encouragement and wisdom provided handholds throughout our journey. Paul Brest's and Hal Harvey's book, *Money Well Spent*, was an invaluable resource to us, as it should be for anyone seriously interested in pursuing philanthropy strategically. Mario Morino, the founder of Venture Philanthropy Partners, contributed an array of practical insights through VPP's robust newsletters and his unvarnished advice. Patty Stonesifer provided early inspiration for this project; her wise counsel and extensive experience dramatically influenced the contours of *Give Smart*. Steve Hilton's generosity and encouragement motivated us during a particularly formative time. Carol Larson, Greg Dees, Phoebe Boyer, and Forrest Berkley read multiple manuscript drafts, brainstormed ideas, and helped us craft engaging philanthropic stories.

A diverse and talented group of philanthropists and nonprofit leaders served as critical readers and/or provided the educational (and entertaining!) examples that flow throughout these pages. Together, they formed an extraordinary virtual team that shaped and propelled *Give Smart*. We are deeply grateful for their efforts: Laura Arrillaga, Carrie Avery, Matt Bannick, Joshua Bekenstein, Shona

Brown, Jennifer Buffett, Bob Buford, Jim Canales, Daniel Cardinali, Jean Case, Charles Collier, William Damon, Steve Denning, Connie Duckworth, Jonathan Fanton, Bob Fisher, John Ford, Bob Gay, Peter Goldberg, Stephen Heintz, John Hood, Katie Hood, JD Hoye, Joanna Jacobson, Pat Lawler, Peter and Carolyn Lynch, Charles MacCormack, Barnaby Marsh, Steven McCormick, Brian Olson, Pierre and Pam Omidyar, William Price, Jeff Raikes, Julian Robertson, Judith Rodin, Nancy Roob, Herb Sandler, Muneer Satter, John Simon, Edward Skloot, Lorie Slutsky, Oswald Stender, Larry and Joyce Stupski, Kelvin Taketa, Mark Tercek, Darren Walker, Jeffrey Walker, Sandy Weill, John Whitehead, and Elaine Wynn.

A number of outstanding organizations contributed disproportionately to our thinking about philanthropy. The Center for Effective Philanthropy and its president Phil Buchanan have been leaders in helping donors increase their impact. The same can be said of The Philanthropy Roundtable led by Adam Meyerson, Grantmakers for Effective Organizations led by Kathleen Enright, the Center on Wealth and Philanthropy at Boston College led by Paul Schervish, Monitor Institute led by Katherine Fulton, the Foundation Strategy Group led by Mark Kramer, and Rockefeller Philanthropy Advisors led by Melissa Berman. Of special note is The Philanthropic Initiative, whose founder Peter Karoff was a thoughtful pioneer in the philanthropic arena and an inspiration for many.

Among the many commentators on philanthropy, two whom we have found especially thought provoking are Sean Stannard-Stockton, whose Tactical Philanthropy blog provides timely commentary on current issues, and Lucy Bernholz, whose blog, Philanthropy 2173: The Business of Giving, is consistently wide ranging and forward looking.

Long before we even had a contract, PublicAffairs became an active partner in this endeavor. We are grateful to Peter Osnos and

Susan Weinberg for their intellectual guidance and unfailing encouragement, and to Lindsay Jones for her tireless and expert editorial support.

Give Smart was shaped by other hands as well. Alison Powell, Bridgespan's philanthropy knowledge manager, kept us abreast of relevant knowledge from others' books and blogs. Regina Maruca worked with us in 2009 as we were starting to conceptualize the book's structure. Jeff Cruikshank helped us write and rewrite the pages that eventually evolved into the final manuscript. Jen Sauvé and Deb Gordon McNeilly created the compelling graphics, while Susan Descheneaux and Christina Crotteau provided much needed administrative assistance.

Give Smart would not have been possible without the generosity of Goldman Sachs through Goldman Sachs Gives and the unwavering leadership of John R. W. Rogers and Dina Habib Powell. Their belief in us, their deep commitment to philanthropic results, their standards of excellence, and their heartfelt desire to do good in the world exceeded any reasonable expectations. They are the best of partners.

We are deeply grateful for the gifts that all of you have given us; your individual contributions to our collective work helped to bring this book to life. If the insights, ideas, and stories contained in these pages truly encourage "philanthropy that gets results," the beneficiaries will be not only the book's readers and its authors, but also—and most important—all those whose lives you will have helped to change for the better. Thank you.

SPECIAL ACKNOWLEDGMENT: NAN STONE

No single individual was more important in the writing of *Give Smart* than Nan Stone.

Nan actively participated in our basic research, including completing dozens of interviews and reviewing countless books, articles, and presentations. She pushed our thinking beyond initial boundaries, synthesizing and clarifying along the way. Any important ideas in this book are hers to share.

Nan also worked as both architect and craftsman, structuring the logic flow within and across chapters, and shaping the paragraphs to bring ideas to life. Her extraordinary ability both to write and to edit allowed her to integrate our words within a tight package. Her penchant for storytelling helped us turn up the "color knob" through captivating examples. She even cracked the code on some of our more stubborn graphics. Critical readers complimented our drafts as being "highly accessible" and "a pleasure to read." This is the direct consequence of Nan's talent, passion, and commitment.

Over the span of two years, Nan led our process—sometimes from in front, and sometimes from behind. Through countless iterations and endless weekends, she never wavered from our goal of making this book as valuable as possible for our readers. Her aim was not just to produce a book, but rather to craft ideas that would be of practical service to those who strive, through their giving, to achieve real results.

To the extent that *Give Smart* achieves that ambition, Nan Stone deserves the credit.

Nan, we are so very grateful.

NOTES

Preface

1. Thomas J. Tierney, "Toward Higher Impact Philanthropy," in *Taking Philanthropy Seriously: Beyond Noble Intentions to Responsible Giving*, ed. William Damon and Susan Verducci (Bloomington: Indiana University Press, 2006), 62–76.

Introduction

1. "Mass-Producing Excellence: Don Fisher's Strategies for Improving Public Schools Nationwide," Philanthropy Roundtable, July 1, 2005, http://www.philanthropyroundtable.org/article.asp?article=747&paper=1&cat=149.

2. Ibid.

3. Stacy Teicher Khadaroo, "Graduation Rate for US High-Schoolers Falls for Second Straight Year," *Christian Science Monitor*, June 10, 2010.

4. KIPP, "About," http://kipp.org/about-kipp; KIPP, "FAQ," http://www.kipp.org/faq.

5. KIPP, "2015 Imperatives," http://www.kipp.org/index.cfm?objectid=1DFD4FF0-AEDD-11DF-8000005056883C4D.

6. KIPP, "KIPP National Partners," http://www.kipp.org/about-kipp/support-kipp/kipp-national-partners.

7. Ann Goggins Gregory and Don Howard, "The Nonprofit Starvation Cycle," *Stanford Social Innovation Review*, Fall 2009, http://www.bridgespan.org/nonprofit-starvation-cycle.aspx.

Chapter 1

1. Ushahidi, "Home," http://www.ushahidi.com.

2. Humanity United, "About Us," http://www.humanityunited
.org/whoweare.

3. Omidyar Network, "Evolution," http:/www.omidyar.com/about
_us/evolution.

4. Waldemar A. Nielsen, *Inside American Philanthropy: The Dramas
of Donorship* (Norman: University of Oklahoma Press, 1996), 39–42.

5. Peter Max Ascoli, *Julius Rosenwald: The Man Who Built Sears Roebuck* (Bloomington: Indiana University Press, 2006), 408.

6. Joel L. Fleishman, J. Scott Kohler, and Steven Schindler, *Casebook for the Foundation: A Great American Secret* (New York: PublicAffairs, 2009).

7. Ibid.

8. Warren Buffett, "Letter to Peter Buffett," June 26, 2006, http://
www.berkshirehathaway.com/donate/pabltr.pdf.

9. Unless otherwise noted, all quotes and paraphrases in this section
are from an April 5, 2010, interview with Jennifer Buffett conducted
by Susan Wolf Ditkoff, Nan Stone, and Tom Tierney.

10. NoVo Foundation, "Mission," http://novofoundation.org/
wordpress/.

11. "Nike, NoVo Foundation Commit $100 million to the Girl
Effect," *Philanthropy News Digest*, May 28, 2008, http://www.
foundationcenter.org/pnd/news/story.jhtml;jsessionid=IWY0JHGZ
IFIJFLAQBQ4CGXD5AAAACI2F?id=215500054.

12. Stupski Foundation, "History," http://www.stupski.org/
history.htm.

13. Accelerate Brain Cancer Cure, "Our Approach," http://abc2
.org/our-approach.

14. All quotes and paraphrases in this section are from a May 10,
2010, interview with Oswald Stender conducted by Allison Murphy
and Nan Stone.

15. Ryan Jimenez, "The Making of a Cultural Icon," Music Center:

Performing Arts Center of Los Angeles County, http://www.music center.org/about/mc40th.html.

16. Friends of the Children, "Duncan Campbell, Friends of the Children Founder, Wins $50,000 Purpose Prize," 2009, http://www.friendsofthechildren.org/portland/documents/Campbell%20 Purpose%20Prize%20Award%20Winner%20Press%20Release.pdf.

17. Friends of the Children, "Friends of the Children Fact Sheet," http://www.friendschildren.org/wp-content/uploads/2010/09/FOTC -Fact-Sheet-9–2010.pdf.

18. Open Society Foundations, http://www.soros.org/about.

19. Peter G. Peterson Foundation, "About Us," http://www.pgpf .org/About.aspx.

20. Melinda French Gates, "Remarks to the Council on Foundations," April 30, 2007, http://www.gatesfoundation.org/speeches -commentary/Pages/melinda-french-gates-2007-foundation-council .aspx.

21. Funding Universe, "The John D. and Catherine T. MacArthur Foundation," http://www.fundinguniverse.com/company-histories/ The-John-D-and-Catherine-T-MacArthur-Foundation-Company -History.html.

22. Waldemar A. Nielsen, *The Golden Donors: A New Anatomy of the Great Foundations* (New York: Truman Talley Books, E. P. Dutton, 1985), 103.

23. Ibid., 100–15.

24. Duke Endowment, "Indenture of Trust," http://www.duke endowment.org/images/stories/downloads/tde/indenture.pdf.

Chapter 2

1. This framework builds on concepts initially developed by Susan Wolf Ditkoff and Susan J. Colby in "Galvanizing Philanthropy," *Harvard Business Review*, November 2009, 108–15.

2. James Irvine Foundation, "Our Mission," http://www.irvine.org/ about-us/mission.

3. James Irvine Foundation, "Youth," http://www.irvine.org/grant making/our-programs/youth.

4. Don Howard and Pat Wu, "Assessing California's Multiple Pathways Field," *Focus* (foundation newsletter), James Irvine Foundation, May 2009, 2.

5. Alliance for Excellent Education, "Fact Sheet: The Impact of Education on Health & Well-being," November 2003 (Washington, DC).

6. Howard and Wu, *Assessing California's Multiple Pathways Field.*

7. James Irvine Foundation, "The Challenge and Opportunity of Offering Linked Learning to California's Out-of-School Youth," September 13, 2010, 2.

8. James Irvine Foundation, "Youth."

9. James Irvine Foundation, "Evaluation: ConnectEd Network of Schools," http://www.irvine.org/evaluation/program-evaluations/connected-network-of-schools.

10. James Irvine Foundation, "The Challenge and Opportunity."

11. Michael Lollar, "Philanthropist Clarence Day Dies, Left Generous Imprint," *The Commercial Appeal,* October 26, 2009, http://www.commercialappeal.com/news/2009/oct/26/philanthropist-clarence-day-dies-after-car-accident/.

12. Youth Villages, http://www.youthvillages.org.

13. Unless otherwise noted, all quotes and paraphrases in this section are from a September 27, 2010, interview with Pat Lawler conducted by Allison Murphy and Nan Stone.

14. Youth Villages, "Transitional Living," http://www.youth villages.org/what-we-do/transitional-living.aspx.

15. Youth Villages, "Transitional Living Program: How It Works," http://www.youthvillages.org/what-we-do/transitional-living/how-it-works.aspx.

16. Youth Villages, "Transitional Living Program: Frequently Asked Questions," http://www.youthvillages.org/what-we-do/transitional-living/frequently-asked-questions-faq.aspx.

17. Joe Nocera, "Self-Made Philanthropists," *New York Times*, March 9, 2008, http://www.nytimes.com/2008/03/09/magazine/

09Sandlers-t.html?_r=1; ProPublica, "About Us," http://www.propublica.org/about/.

18. Unless otherwise noted, all quotes and paraphrases in this section are from a May 11, 2010, interview with Herb Sandler conducted by Nan Stone and Tom Tierney.

19. Tracy Weber and Charles Ornstein, "Schwarzenegger Replaces Most of State Nursing Board," ProPublica, July 13, 2009, http://www.propublica.org/article/schwarzenegger-replaces-most-of-state-nursing-board-713.

20. Unless otherwise noted, all quotes and paraphrases in this section are from the Draper Richards Foundation Web site, http://www.draperrichards.org.

21. Unless otherwise noted, the information in this section is from the Barbara Lee Family Foundation Web site, http://www.barbaraleefoundation.org.

22. All quotes and paraphrases in this section are from a November 16, 2010, interview with Adrienne Kimmell conducted by Nan Stone.

23. All quotes and paraphrases in this section are from a February 24, 2010, Bridgespan interview with a Maine philanthropist.

24. Maine Community Foundation, "Stand Up and Be Counted: To Magnify His Philanthropy, a Maine CF Donor Turns to Challenges," *Maine Ties: News from the Maine Community Foundation*, Winter 2010.

25. All quotes and paraphrases in this section are from a March 15, 2010, interview with Jeff Walker conducted by Susan Wolf Ditkoff, Allison Murphy, and Nan Stone.

26. NPower, "About Us," http://www.npower.org/about.

27. Michael J. Fox Foundation, "About Michael," http://www.michaeljfox.org/about_aboutMichael.cfm.

28. All quotes and paraphrases in this section are from a March 24, 2010, interview with Katie Hood conducted by Susan Wolf Ditkoff.

29. The Annenberg Challenge, "About the Annenbert Challenge," http://www.annenberginstitute.org/challenge/about/about.html.

30. Ibid.

31. Joel L. Fleishman, *The Foundation: A Great American Secret* (New York: Public Affairs, 2009), 267–68.

32. Annenberg Institute for School Reform, http://www.annenberg institute.org.

Chapter 3

1. Stanford professor William Damon, in a 2004 conversation with Joel Fleishman, concluded that "the conservative foundations went about education reform in the right way. They supported a number of people to write about the idea of vouchers and charter schools and did not immediately try to implement any of the ideas massively."

2. United Way, "History," http://liveunited.org/pages/history.

3. Edna McConnell Clark Foundation, "Growth Capital Aggregation Pilot," http://www.emcf.org/how-we-work/growth-capital-aggregation-pilot/.

4. Climate Works Foundation, http://climateworks.org; Marty Michaels, "Grant Makers Pour More Than $1-Billion Into Climate-Change Crusade, *The Chronicle of Philanthropy*, April 9, 2009, http://philanthropy.com/article/Grant-Makers-Pour-More-Than/56848/.

5. Andrew Jack, "Gates' Charity to Shift Stance on Hand-Outs," *Financial Times*, September 22, 2009, http://www.ft.com/cms/s/0/f93b6b00-a7a0-11de-b0ee-00144feabdc0.html.

6. Bill & Melinda Gates Foundation, "Aspire Public Schools Secures $90 Million Bond Financing for Permanent Facilities with Guarantees from Gates and Charles and Helen Schwab Foundations," May 6, 2010, http://www.gatesfoundation.org/press-releases/Pages/expanding-aspire-public-schools-pri-100506.aspx.

7. New York City Housing Authority, "About," http://www.nyc.gov/html/nycha/html/about/about.shtml.

8. New York City Housing Authority, "The Plan to Preserve Public Housing," April 2006, http://www.nyc.gov/html/nycha/downloads/pdf/ppph-eng.pdf.

9. The City of New York, "The New Housing Marketplace: Creating Housing for the Next Generation," http://www.nyc.gov/html/hpd/downloads/pdf/10yearHMplan.pdf.

10. Omidyar Network, http://www.omidyar.com/.

11. All quotes and paraphrases in this section are from a May 10, 2010, interview with Matt Bannick and Sarah Steven conducted by Susan Wolf Ditkoff, Nan Stone, and Tom Tierney.

12. Ann Hornaday, "For the Studio Behind 'Waiting for Superman,' Movies Are a Tool for Change," *Washington Post*, October 3, 2010, http://www.washingtonpost.com/wp-dyn/content/article/2010/10/01/AR2010100103174.html?hpid=sec-artsliving.

13. Participant Media, "Our History," http://www.participant media.com/company/history.php.

14. Hornaday, "For the Studio."

15. Dan Milmo and David Adam, "Branson Pledges $3bn Transport Profits to Fight Global Warming," *Guardian*, September 22, 2006, http://www.guardian.co.uk/environment/2006/sep/22/travelnews.frontpagenews.

16. Kleiner Perkins Caufield & Byers, "Kleiner Perkins Caufield & Byers Launches Green Growth Fund," May 1, 2008, http://www.kpcb.com/news/articles/2008_05_00.html.

17. All quotes and paraphrases in this section are from an April 27, 2010, interview with Peter Lynch conducted by Nan Stone and Tom Tierney.

18. All quotes and paraphrases in this section are from a March 29, 2010, interview with Lynch Foundation executive director Katie Everett conducted by Allison Murphy.

19. All quotes and paraphrases in this section are from a July 22, 2010, interview with Muneer Satter conducted by Allison Murphy, Nan Stone, and Tom Tierney.

20. New Profit Inc., http://www.newprofit.com.

21. All quotes and paraphrases in this section are from a March 12, 2010, interview with Josh Bekenstein conducted by Nan Stone and Tom Tierney.

22. All quotes and paraphrases in this section are from a September 14, 2010, interview with JD Hoye and Sandy Weill conducted by Allison Murphy and Nan Stone.

23. Ralph T. King, "Ray of Hope," *Wall Street Journal* (Eastern edition), September 30, 1992.

24. All quotes and paraphrases in this section are from an April 21, 2010, interview with Jean Case conducted by Allison Murphy, Nan Stone, and Tom Tierney.

25. Network for Good, "About Us," http://www1.networkforgood.org/about-us.

26. Case Foundation, "Make It Your Own Awards," http://www.casefoundation.org/projects/make-it-your-own-awards.

27. Lasker Foundation, "Foundation History," http://www.laskerfoundation.org/about/history.htm.

28. Jeffrey L. Cruikshank and Arthur W. Schultz, *The Man Who Sold America* (Boston: Harvard Business Review Press, 2010), 355.

29. All quotes and paraphrases in this section are from a March 24, 2010, interview with Darren Walker conducted by Susan Wolf Ditkoff.

30. Rockefeller Foundation, "Who We Are, Rebuilding New Orleans," http://www.rockefellerfoundation.org/who-we-are/what-we-are-learning/rebuilding-new-orleans.

31. Interview with Jean Case (see note 24).

32. Joel L. Fleishman, J. Scott Kohler, and Steven Schindler, *Casebook for the Foundation: A Great American Secret* (New York: Public Affairs, 2009).

33. Nobelprize.org, "Norman Borlaug," http://nobelprize.org/nobel_prizes/peace/laureates/1970/borlaug-bio.html.

34. All quotes and paraphrases in this section are from an October 1, 2010, interview with Carrie Avery conducted by Susan Wolf Ditkoff and Allison Murphy.

Chapter 4

1. All quotes and paraphrases in this section are from a July 7, 2010, interview with Margaret Hall and John Simon conducted by Susan Wolf Ditkoff, Allison Murphy, Nan Stone, and Tom Tierney.

2. Jim Collins, *Good to Great* (New York: HarperBusiness, 2001).

3. This comment was made to Tom Tierney in the course of a con-

sulting engagement by a nonprofit leader who wished to remain anonymous.

4. Daniel Stid and Jeffrey L. Bradach, "How Visionary Nonprofit Leaders Are Learning to Enhance Management Capabilities," *Strategy & Leadership* 37, no. 1 (2009), http://www.bridgespan.org/learning center/resourcedetail.aspx?id=312.

5. Kirk Kramer and Daniel Stid, "The Effective Organization: Five Questions to Translate Leadership into Strong Management," The Bridgespan Group, May 3, 2010, http://www.bridgespan.org/ LearningCenter/ResourceDetail.aspx?id=2624.

6. Unless otherwise noted, all quotes and paraphrases in this section are from an August 16, 2010, interview with John Whitehead conducted by Nan Stone and Tom Tierney.

7. Unless otherwise noted, all quotes and paraphrases in this section are from an October 1, 2010, interview with Carrie Avery conducted by Susan Wolf Ditkoff and Allison Murphy.

8. The Durfee Foundation, "Sabbatical Program," http://www. durfee.org/programs/sabbatical/index.html.

9. Deborah S. Linnell and Tim Wolfred, "Creative Disruption: Sabbaticals for Capacity Building and Leadership Development in the Nonprofit Sector," 2009, http://www.durfee.org/programs/sabbatical /reports.html.

10. Ibid.

11. Ann Goggins Gregory and Don Howard, "The Nonprofit Starvation Cycle."

Chapter 5

1. Unless otherwise noted, all quotes and paraphrases in this section are from a July 28, 2010, interview with Nancy Roob conducted by Allison Murphy and Nan Stone.

2. Unless otherwise noted, the quotes related to Youth Villages' experience in this section are from a September 27, 2010, interview with Pat Lawler conducted by Allison Murphy and Nan Stone.

3. Youth Villages, "Youth Villages Outcomes for All Programs," http://www.youthvillages.org/how-we-succeed/outcome-driven-approach/outcomes-all-programs.aspx; Youth Villages, "Youth Villages' Programs July 2000 through September 2010," http://www.youthvillages.org/LinkClick.aspx?fileticket=70W1lDMAROM%3d&tabid=620.

4. Tipping Point Community, "Funding Criteria," http://www.tippingpoint.org/index.php?option=com_content&view=article&id=88&Itemid=72.

5. All quotes and paraphrases in this section are from a July 22, 2010 Bridgespan interview with a philanthropist.

6. Source Watch, "John Olin Foundation Mission," http://www.sourcewatch.org/index.php?title=John_M._Olin_Foundation.

7. John J. Miller, *Strategic Investment in Ideas: How Two Foundations Reshaped America* (Washington, DC: The Philanthropy Roundtable, 2003).

8. John J. Miller, *A Gift of Freedom: How the John M. Olin Foundation Changed America* (San Francisco: Encounter Books, 2006).

9. Unless otherwise noted, all quotes and paraphrases regarding the Gordon and Betty Moore Foundation can be found on their Web site, http://www.moore.org.

10. Gulf of Maine Research Institute, "About GRMI," http://gmri.org/about/index.asp.

11. Gordon and Betty Moore Foundation, "Program That Fosters Open Dialogue around Fishery Management in the Gulf of Maine Gains National Support," November 15, 2006, http://www.moore.org/newsitem.aspx?id=1860.

12. All quotes and paraphrases in this section are from an April 27, 2010, interview with Peter Lynch conducted by Nan Stone and Tom Tierney.

13. All quotes and paraphrases in this section are from a June 3, 2010, interview with Carolyn Lynch conducted by Allison Murphy and Nan Stone.

14. This comment was made to Tom Tierney in the course of a

consulting engagement by a nonprofit leader who wished to remain anonymous.

15. All quotes and paraphrases in this section are from a July 27, 2010, interview with Dan Cardinali and Elaine Wynn conducted by Allison Murphy and Nan Stone.

16. Communities in Schools, http://www.cis-pa.org/.

17. Communities in Schools, "President's Message," *Inside CIS* 5, no. 3 (June 2010). http://communitiesinschools.org/static/media/uploads/attachments/Inside_CIS_June_2010.pdf.

18. Communities in Schools and IFC International, "The Communities in Schools National Evaluation: Mid-Level Findings," 2008, http://www.communitiesinschools.org/static/media/uploads/attachments/The_Communities_In_Schools_National_Evaluation_Mid-Level_Findings.pdf.

19. Ellie Buteau, Phil Buchanan, and Timothy Chu, "Working with Grantees: The Keys to Success and Five Program Officers Who Exemplify Them," Center for Effective Philanthropy, 2010, http://www.effectivephilanthropy.org/assets/pdfs/CEP_Working_with_Grantees.pdf.

20. All quotes and paraphrases in this section are from an October 4, 2010, interview with Ally Burns and Jean Case conducted by Allison Murphy, Nan Stone, and Tom Tierney.

21. All quotes and paraphrases in this section are from an April 26, 2010, interview with Brian Olson conducted by Nan Stone and Tom Tierney.

Chapter 6

1. This comment was made to Tom Tierney in the course of a consulting engagement by a philanthropist who wished to remain anonymous.

2. All quotes and paraphrases in this section are from an August 9, 2010, interview with Steve Hilton conducted by Allison Murphy, Nan Stone, and Tom Tierney.

3. Conrad N. Hilton Foundation, "Last Will and Testament," http://www.hiltonfoundation.org/about/last-will.

4. This comment was made to Tom Tierney in the course of a consulting engagement by a philanthropist who wished to remain anonymous.

5. Mario Morino, "Social Outcomes: Missing the Forest for the Trees?" Venture Philosophy Partners, January 8, 2010, http://www.vppartners.org/learning/perspectives/corner/0110_social-outcomes.html.

6. Jim Collins, *Good to Great* (New York: Harper Business, 2001).

7. All quotes and paraphrases in this section are from a July 19, 2010, interview with Connie Duckworth conducted by Susan Wolf Ditkoff, Allison Murphy, Nan Stone, and Tom Tierney.

8. Arzu Studio Hope, http://www.arzurugs.org.

9. WHO, UNICEF, UNFPA, and the World Bank, "Trends in Maternal Mortality: 1990 to 2008," Childinfo, http://www.childinfo.org/files/Trends_in_Maternal_Mortality_1990_to_2008.pdf.

10. Gill Foundation, http://www.gillfoundation.org/.

11. Ellie Buteau et al., "Essentials of Foundation Strategy," Center for Effective Philanthropy, December 2009, http://www.effective philanthropy.org/assets/pdfs/CEP_EssentialsOfFoundationStrategy.pdf.

12. "A Decade of Progress on LGBT Rights," Movement Advancement Project, http://www.lgbtmap.org/file/a-decade-of-lgbt-progress.pdf.

13. David and Lucile Packard Foundation, "What We Fund," http://www.packard.org/categoryList.aspx?RootCatID=3&CategoryID=61.

14. Susan Wolf Ditkoff and Susan Colby, "Galvanizing Philanthropy," *Harvard Business Review*, November 2009, which is based on consulting engagements with the Packard Foundation.

15. Ibid.

16. All quotes and paraphrases in this section are from an August 18, 2010, interview with JD Hoye conducted by Allison Murphy and Nan Stone.

17. All quotes and paraphrases in this section are from an October 20, 2010, interview with Jeff Raikes conducted by Nan Stone and Tom Tierney.

18. Jeff Raikes, "Grantee Perception Report Summary," Bill & Melinda Gates Foundation, June 15, 2010, http://www.gates foundation.org/learning/Pages/grantee-perception-report.aspx.

19. "Know Where You're Going: An Interview with Hewlett President Paul Brest," Philanthropy Roundtable, January 1, 2004, http://www.philanthropyroundtable.org/article.asp?article=861&paper=1&cat=149.

20. John J. Havens and Paul G. Schervish, "Why the $41 Trillion Wealth Transfer Estimate Is Still Valid: A Review of Challenges and Questions," *The Journal of Gift Planning* 7, no. 1 (January 2003): 11–15, 47–50.

21. The Giving Pledge, http://www.givingpledge.org.

22. Bridgespan analysis based on the research of John J. Havens and Paul G. Schervish of the Boston College Center on Wealth and Philanthropy and other sources.

23. Naomi Schaefer Riley, "What They're Doing after Harvard," *Wall Street Journal*, July 10, 2010, http://online.wsj.com/article/SB10001424052748704198004575311052522926796.html.

24. David Simms and Carol Trager, "Report: Finding Leaders for America's Nonprofits," The Bridgespan Group, April 20 2009, http://www.bridgespan.org/finding-leaders-for-americas-nonprofits.aspx?Resource=Articles.

INDEX

Thomas J. Tierney is the cofounder and chairman of The Bridgespan Group, a nonprofit consulting firm serving the nonprofit sector and philanthropists. Prior to founding Bridgespan, Mr. Tierney served as managing partner worldwide of Bain & Company from June 1992 to January 2000.

Joel L. Fleishman is professor of law and public policy at Duke University. The author of *The Foundation,* he has served as president of the Atlantic Philanthropic Service Company, the U.S. program staff of Atlantic Philanthropies.

PublicAffairs is a publishing house founded in 1997. It is a tribute to the standards, values, and flair of three persons who have served as mentors to countless reporters, writers, editors, and book people of all kinds, including me.

I. F. Stone, proprietor of *I. F. Stone's Weekly,* combined a commitment to the First Amendment with entrepreneurial zeal and reporting skill and became one of the great independent journalists in American history. At the age of eighty, Izzy published *The Trial of Socrates,* which was a national bestseller. He wrote the book after he taught himself ancient Greek.

Benjamin C. Bradlee was for nearly thirty years the charismatic editorial leader of *The Washington Post.* It was Ben who gave the *Post* the range and courage to pursue such historic issues as Watergate. He supported his reporters with a tenacity that made them fearless, and it is no accident that so many became authors of influential, best-selling books.

Robert L. Bernstein, the chief executive of Random House for more than a quarter century, guided one of the nation's premier publishing houses. Bob was personally responsible for many books of political dissent and argument that challenged tyranny around the globe. He is also the founder and was the longtime chair of Human Rights Watch, one of the most respected human rights organizations in the world.

.   .   .

For fifty years, the banner of Public Affairs Press was carried by its owner Morris B. Schnapper, who published Gandhi, Nasser, Toynbee, Truman, and about 1,500 other authors. In 1983 Schnapper was described by *The Washington Post* as "a redoubtable gadfly." His legacy will endure in the books to come.

Peter Osnos, *Founder and Editor-at-Large*